THE MURDER OF
MARILYN MONROE

THE MURDER OF MARILYN MONROE

Leonore Canevari, Jeanette van Wyhe, Christian Dimas, and Rachel Dimas

With a foreword and afterword by Brad Steiger

Carroll & Graf Publishers/Richard Gallen
New York

DEDICATION

To Marilyn . . . who remains larger than life even in death. She asked for our help to set the record straight, and based on the detailed information made available to us, we have fulfilled our promise to her. Our fond hope is that with the release of *The Murder of Marilyn Monroe* she will finally be free to move on.

. . . And to the spirit friends we made, especially Peter, who helped us with our mission, "Goodbye . . . we will miss you."

ACKNOWLEDGMENTS

The authors wish to thank Leverett Boruszak for the kindness and patience she extended to us. Her artistic talent produced drawings from only our vivid recall of the faces we had seen in our visualizations.

A thank-you also to Mrs. Valerie DeSimas for helping us in beginning our research.

CONTENTS

. . . AND A SOUL CRIES OUT FOR JUSTICE

When Marilyn Monroe died on the morning of August 5, 1962, her death was immediately enshrouded with mystery and controversy, and she joined the ranks of such movie stars as Jean Harlow, Lupe Velez, George Reeves, and subsequently Bruce Lee and Natalie Wood, whose deaths are clouded by allegations of suicide or murder.

Few of Harlow's fans accepted the official studio decree of death due to uremic poisoning. Those who vicariously savored the erotic adventures of Lupe Velez were reluctant to acknowledge the Mexican spitfire's forlorn suicide note. Loyal fans continue to believe that television "Superman" George Reeves was the victim of murder, rather than depression. And followers of real-life superman Bruce Lee "know" that he was assassinated by the secret Kung Fu society of the Black

Hand. The official account of the drowning of Natalie Wood, according to her star worshippers, simply contains too many contradictions and unacceptable elements to be ever considered an accidental death.

Although Marilyn Monroe's fits of temperament and bouts of depression were well publicized and a drug overdose would seem a probable cause of death, the final verdict that she died by her own hand has never been acceptable to millions of her devoted fans or to hundreds of skeptical investigators. Those who firmly express their doubts that the actress committed suicide have suggested that she may have been murdered to silence her accounts of steamy sexual affairs with no less than the President of the United States, John F. Kennedy, and his brother Robert, the nation's attorney general.

Before we examine the startling scenario presented by this remarkable new book, *The Murder of Marilyn Monroe*, we need to establish the facts of Marilyn Monroe's death as we have previously understood them.

It was around 3:00 A.M. on the morning of August 5, 1962, when Marilyn Monroe's housekeeper, Mrs. Eunice Murray, noticed that there was still light in the actress's bedroom and decided to inquire why she was not yet asleep. Mrs. Murray's concern grew when she found that the bedroom door was locked and she was unable to receive any type of response from her employer.

Summoned by Mrs. Murray, Marilyn's psychiatrist, Dr. Ralph Greenson, arrived at the actress's Spanish-style bungalow in less than half an hour. After his own unsuccessful attempt to rouse Marilyn by rapping loudly on the bedroom door, Dr. Greenson grabbed a poker from the fireplace and used it to smash a bedroom window. He found his famous patient lying naked in bed, covered with a blanket and a sheet. She clutched the telephone receiver in a lifeless hand.

Dr. Hyman Engelberg, the actress's personal physician, arrived within the hour to pronounce the cinematic goddess officially dead. It had been Dr. Engelberg who had prescribed the sleeping medications on which it seemed Marilyn had overdosed. Every reader of movie fan magazines was well aware of Marilyn's celebrated bouts of insomnia. On this fateful evening, her wish to sleep had been ultimately fulfilled.

Before 5:00 A.M. Detective R. E. Byron and two police officers had examined the death room and the entire house and decided that they could find nothing that would indicate any act of violence perpetrated upon the deceased. They noted the twelve to fifteen bottles of various medicines clustered on a night table near the star's bed.

Two deputy coroners arrived to wrap Marilyn Monroe's body in a pale-blue blanket and strap it onto a stretcher. The corpse was placed in a station wagon and transported to the Westwood Village Mortuary. Later, it was transferred to the county morgue for the coroner's inquest and the official ruling regarding the cause of death—an overdose of barbiturates, a possible suicide. The reigning love goddess of the Hollywood screen was dead at the age of thirty-six.

Over the past thirty years, books, plays, motion pictures, and television productions have presented possible scenarios for the manner in which one of the most powerful families in the nation may have ordered the death of one of the most popular love goddesses in the movies. An almost equal number of presentations have protested the outrageousness of accusing the Kennedy family of having Marilyn Monroe killed in order to eliminate a potential scandal. With undeniable assertions, the Kennedy defenders remind us of the actress's monumental temper tantrums, her much-publicized bouts of depression, her apparent emotional instability.

But now new evidence has been set forth that states unequivocally that Marilyn Monroe was murdered. The assassins are named and described. The events leading to the foul deed are revealed in painful detail. Every question that anyone might wish to ask regarding the method and means of murder are answered. What is more, the damning testimony comes from Marilyn Monroe herself!

Has a hitherto unrevealed tape recording of the terrible event been discovered? A diary, perhaps? Or a bizarre kind of last will and testament?

No, what we have here in this remarkable book are the transcripts of a series of contacts that the authors Leonore Canevari, Jeanette van Wyhe, Christian Dimas, and Rachel Dimas had with a spirit that they believe was Marilyn Monroe. Beginning with a session on June 8, 1990, the mediumistic authors, members of the Association for Paranormal Investigation of Fresno, California, pursued their otherworldly interviews until they attained what they felt to be an in-depth rapport with Marilyn Monroe's spirit. In addition, they carefully researched and documented to the best of their ability each new scrap of testimony and evidence that the entity presented to them.

The authors of *The Murder of Marilyn Monroe* are convinced that the communicating entity who provided them with intimate details of the screen goddess's life and her tragic death was, in fact, the surviving spiritual essence of Marilyn Monroe. They believe her protestations that she did not commit suicide and they accept her testimony that she was murdered according to a death sentence decreed in 1962 by two of the most powerful men in America.

But even as the readers of this book may be willing to respect the authors' belief construct, they will undoubtedly be asking such persistent questions as whether or not the entire process of making contact with the alleged spirit of a deceased personality—regardless of having received ostensibly accurate information—was not some kind of collective delusion? Also, is it possible to trust any information that has been obtained in alleged dialogue with the spirit of a person who is known to be deceased and discarnate?

The literature of psychical research provides us with hundreds of examples in which people received information that not only proved to be trustworthy, but that also brought about productive resolutions, discoveries, knowledge, even great wealth. It would take a book of prodigious size to do scant justice to an even cursory sampling of such cases, but for the purposes of illustration, we shall cite only the few that follow:

*Abraham Lincoln, one of the most revered Presidents of the United States, was constantly chided by the newspapers of his time for his consultations with the spirit world. Lincoln himself spoke of the "wonderful things" that he had witnessed during seances held in the White House, and he admitted that the messages he had received from the spirit entities had enabled him to come through crisis after crisis. Lincoln sometimes felt himself in contact with the entity of Daniel Webster, and there is some evidence that his championing the Emancipation Proclamation was spirit-inspired.

*In 1908, the discovery of Edgar Chapel, long buried and forgotten in the ruins of the diocese of Bath and Wells in England, was accomplished after the spirit of a monk named Johannes, who claimed to have lived from 1497 to 1534, communicated to F. Bligh Bond, an architect, the precise directions as to where to begin to excavate. The monk utilized the hand of Captain J. Allen Bartlett to write a detailed description of the chapel in medieval English and in Latin.

*Before Arthur Edward Stilwell died on September 26, 1928, he had built the Kansas City Southern Railroad; the Kansas City Northern Connecting Railroad; the Kansas City, Omaha and Eastern; the Kansas City, Omaha and Orient; the Pittsburg and Gulf Railroad; and the Port Arthur Ship Canal. This hardheaded, practical businessman had been responsible for the laying of over twenty-five hundred miles of double-track railroad and the founding of forty towns. He employed over two hundred fifty thousand people in an empire that extended itself past the gigantic railroad network into pecan farming, banking, land development, and mining. In his spare time, Stilwell wrote and published thirty books, nineteen of which were novels, among them the well known *Light That Never Failed.*

Hailed as a genius with unquenchable luck, Stilwell never took any of the credit for his impressive accomplishments as a modern-day Midas. Ever since he had been a boy on his father's farm in eastern Indiana, Arthur Stilwell had received guidance from the spirits of three engineers, a poet, and two writers.

*In 1933, the famous British medium Estelle Roberts received a communication from the spirit of Bessy Manning, who gave the exact address of her mother so that the medium could write Mrs. Manning a letter filled with intimate details that only Bessy and she could have known. Prior to the spirit contact, Mrs. Roberts had never met or corresponded with any member of the Manning family.

*On September 3, 1967, during a telecast on CTV, Toronto, Ontario, Canada, Episcopal Bishop James A. Pike received messages from his deceased son through the mediumship of the Reverend Arthur Ford, an ordained minister of the Disciples of Christ Church. During the same program, Bishop Pike was given additional messages from a number of people on the Other Side who had been important in the development of his life's work as a clergyman.

In a subsequent interview with the Associated Press, Bishop Pike stated that no research done by Reverend Ford could have turned up such intimate details and facts about his life and the individuals who had shaped his thinking.

Is it really possible to communicate with the dead?

For those who answer in the affirmative, they will find that they are by no means alone and that they stand in very good company.

For those who deny such ethereal communication, it might interest them to learn just how many people accept the reality of meaningful interaction with deceased personalities who now exist in another dimension of reality.

In the fall of 1988, the editors at *Better Homes and Gardens* decided to broach a subject they had never before touched: their readers' spiritual lives. They were amazed at both the quantity and the substance of the response to their survey. Editor-in-Chief David Jordan commented that while the publication reached around thirty-six million readers each month, they could usually expect a response of around twenty-five thousand to the surveys that they published. "But this subject," he said, "drew more than eighty thousand responses, and more than ten thousand people attached thoughtful letters."

Pertinent to our immediate interest, 89 percent of the respondents believed in eternal life; 30 percent perceived an astral realm in which spirits might reside; 13 percent accepted the possibility of channeling messages from the spirit world.

In a Gallup poll of a few years back, 43 percent of those surveyed reported an unusual spiritual experience and 71 percent believed in life after death.

Father Andrew Greeley, who is also a Ph.D. in sociology and a best-selling novelist, released very interesting data on the paranormal experiences of Americans in the January/February 1987 issue of *American Health*. According to this survey, conducted by the University of Chicago and the University of Arizona in Tucson, 42 percent of the adult population in the United States believed that they have been in contact with the dead; 73 percent acknowledged the reality of life after death; and 67 percent experienced some manifestation of ESP.

In the mid-1980's, thousands of men and women found themselves sudden participants in a spiritual revolution that swept the planet. People from all walks of life—college professors, doctors, business executives, housewives, truck drivers, and common laborers—became regular conduits for messages from entities who allegedly communicated from other worlds or other dimensions. The mechanism of channeling enabled ordinary people to do things in an extraordinary way. They made contact with a source of power and inspiration outside themselves; they were elevated to higher realms of consciousness and communion with unseen beings. Throughout the world, people were expressing what may be an innate human ability to channel personal guidance from a nonphysical plane of a greater reality.

The explosion of interest in channeling popularized by the Academy Award-winning actress Shirley MacLaine in such books as *Out on a Limb* and demonstrated by such mediums as Kevin Ryerson and J. Z. Knight may be a rediscovery of personal shamanism. Coupled with the awareness that we are all multidimensional beings, the individual shamanic impulse to communicate with the world of spirits may have reemerged within the human psyche with a power that would not be denied by our nuclear-age technology.

Those men and women with psychic or mediumistic abilities, such as the authors of *The Murder of Marilyn Monroe*—Leonore Canevari, Jeanette van Wyhe, Christian Dimas, and Rachel Dimas—have been studied in all earnestness and seriousness in parapsychological laboratories for well over one hundred years. Most parapsychologists believe that the difference between those with genuine mediumistic talents and the great majority of humankind lies in the fact that the psychic sensitive's threshold of consciousness is set lower than that of others. In other words, the psychic sensitive has access to levels of awareness that lie beyond normal reach in the subconscious.

Spirit mediums usually work in trance. While in this state of altered consciousness, the mediums feel that they are under the direction of a spirit guide or control. Spiritists believe in the reality of the guide as a spiritual entity apart from the medium.

Many readers who are familiar with spirit seances only through rather flamboyant or melodramatic scenes in motion pictures or television productions may be quite curious as to the procedures involved in the process of making spirit contact. The phenomena of the seance room generally fit within the categories of clairvoyance, clairaudience, telepathy, automatic writing, percussive sounds (spirit raps), movement of objects (psychokinesis), and the materialization of spirit forms. The medium may go into deep trance, during which state a spirit guide assumes control, and what is known as "direct voice" mediumship occurs. There is also the "twilight trance," during which the medium retains control and may converse with the guide; or no trance at all, during which questions may be put directly to the clairvoyant faculties of the medium.

The mediums who have authored *The Murder of Marilyn Monroe* have utilized a Ouija board and the moving of a planchette to spell out the messages from the spirit of the deceased actress. For those unfamiliar with its workings, the Ouija board is an instrument composed of a flat board and a movable planchette, a heart-shaped pointer. Although there are various shapes and designs, most boards have the alphabet, the numerals one to ten, and the words "yes" and "no" printed on their faces. The hand(s) of the medium rests lightly upon the planchette as spirit control moves the pointer from letter to letter to spell out messages. Some authorities state that such devices date back to the days of Pythagoras, around 540 B.C.

In addition to the Ouija board used by these authors to establish contact with the spirit of Marilyn Monroe, it seems that there is also a direct telepathic linkup with the spirit essence of the actress which permits certain of their group to achieve a dramatic visualization of the events that the spirit describes.

All who have witnessed, under test conditions, any of the phenomena of the seance room, usually acknowledge the functioning of a dynamic force capable of yielding information that could not have been learned by the medium via the normal channels of sensory impressions. The spiritistic thesis holds that this intelligence emanates from the dead.

One soon discovers that the best manner in which to secure a demonstration of genuine spiritistic phenomena is to assure the medium of one's good will. When one has the confidence of the medium, one has gone a long way toward creating harmonious conditions, an indispensable prerequisite to the production of genuine phenomena.

If the reader should attend a seance to judge such manifestations for himself or herself, he should be certain to give the medium to understand that he, as sitter, is assured of the medium's honesty and of his ability to produce genuine phenomena. He should not hurry the medium, but allow him to take all the time he wishes. The neophyte sitter should remember that the greatest guarantee of a successful seance is the medium's serene state of mind.

If one should attend a seance in which no phenomena is produced, he should not conclude that the medium is therefore dishonest. Psychism is not easily turned on and off like a radio or television set. By no means, of course, should one condone outright fraud on the part of a professional medium, but until the natural laws governing this kind of phenomena are better understood, it would seem not only charitable but just to reserve the charges of trickery only for those instances in which gimmicked paraphernalia have been found to have been prepared by the medium in advance of the seance.

Why are so many people reluctant to accept the possibility of spirit communication? Certainly our modern materialistic and mechanistic science has done much to obliterate the idea of soul and the duality of mind and body. The concept of mind-soul has been replaced by an emphasis on brain cells, conditioned responses, and memory patterns. For such scientists as the parapsychologists, who still contend that man and mind are something other than physical things, extensive studies have demonstrated the enormous reach and ability of the human psyche. Parapsychologists have accumulated evidence indicating that the human mind is capable of projecting a segment of its psyche unhampered by time and space, that one level of the mind may be able to give "birth" to new personalities, that one level of the subconscious may telepathically gain knowledge of the deceased from a person's memories. Paradoxically, the more parapsychologists have learned about the range and power of the human mind, the less credence they have given to mediumistic proof of survival.

Certain parapsychologists have observed that the intelligences exhibited by the "spirits" seem most often to be on a level with that of the medium through which they manifest themselves. These investigators admit that the information relayed often rises above the medium's known objective knowledge, but they are quick to point out that the limits of the subjective human mind are not yet known.

Other critics of spiritistic phenomena also point out that the "spirits" can sometimes be controlled by the power of suggestion and can be made to respond to questions that have no basis in reality. Certain researchers have discovered that one can almost as readily establish communication with an imaginary person on the Other Side as with a real one.

In spite of the opposition of their peers, an impressive roster of many of the world's best minds have been vitally concerned with psychical research and have believed that spirit communication is both possible and achievable. Sir John Eccles, winner of the 1963 Nobel Prize in Physiology/Medicine for his pioneering work on the communication of nerve cells, openly declared his belief in a nonmaterial and aware "self" that enters our brain sometime during embryological development or early childhood. This nonmaterial self—the "ghost in the machine," as Arthur Koestler called it—imbues us with everything that makes us distinctly human: self-awareness, free will, personal identity, creativity, the emotions. What is more, Eccles maintained, this "ghost" survives after the physical machine dies.

Pierre Curie, who with his wife Marie discovered radium, stated his opinion that psychical research had more importance than any other field of scientific inquiry. Freud, the father of psychoanalysis, expressed a similar opinion, and Carl Jung remained actively involved in psychic experiences until his death.

Sir Arthur Conan Doyle, creator of Sherlock Holmes, became so obsessed with psychical research that he "killed off" his famous fictional character in order to devote his full time to the Society for Psychical Research. The Nobel Prize-winning poet Yeats was outspoken in discussing his own paranormal experiences. Aldous Huxley wrote a number of books dealing with psychic phenomena.

Sir William Crookes, the great physicist, conducted an exhaustive study of psychic phenomena. The German philosopher Schopenhauer insisted that such phenomena were the most important aspects of human experience and that it was the obligation of every scientist to know more about them. Julian Huxley, the biologist; Sir James Jeans, the astronomer; Arnold Toynbee, the historian; Alfred North Whitehead, the philosopher; William James, the psychologist—all concerned themselves with psychical research.

To continue only briefly with a listing of those famous people of achievement who have believed in the promise of psychical research would be to continue to name a virtual "Who's Who" of the world's greatest thinkers. Thomas A. Edison not only believed in spirit communication, but was working on an electronic apparatus to facilitate such contact at the time of his death. Benjamin Franklin, statesman and inventor; Henry Ford, inventor and entrepreneur; and publishing magnate William Randolph Hearst all firmly believed in an afterlife. Military strategist General George S. Patton and J. Paul Getty, the oil billionaire, accepted the reality of spirit contact.

Aviation pioneer Charles Lindbergh made his historic flight across the Atlantic Ocean together with ghostly human presences who helped to guide him to safety. Ernest Thompson Seton, one of the founders of the Boy Scouts; author Mark Twain; philosopher Henry David Thoreau; and poet Walt Whitman all celebrated their spirits eternal and their contact with personalities who had preceded them to the Other Side.

Isn't it completely logical that our greatest minds are concerned with psychical research and the possibility that we can communicate with entities in the spirit world? What is more central to the core of humankind's existence than the question of survival after death? To be able to prove that the Essential Self within each human entity transcends physical death would at last be able to provide the final answer to the ancient query, "If a man die, shall he live again?"

The idea that there is something within the human mechanism that survives physical death, that some part of our being is immortal, profoundly affects the lives of those who harbor such a belief. The orthodox religions promise their congregations a life eternal, but it cannot be denied that many men and women base their hope for a life beyond the grave on the evidence for survival that has been produced by psychical research.

In spite of the fact that psychic sensitives and mediums have been condemned as cultists, scorned as satanists, and reprimanded for communing with "evil spirits," most of them have become remarkably thick-skinned toward their vociferous critics. Psychic sensitives remain puzzled by the lack of logic demonstrated by members of orthodox religions who say that it is all right to hope for survival, but wrong to prove it.

Although certain investigators argue that such spontaneous evidence as that provided by psychics can never prove anything scientifically because the phenomena produced cannot be repeated under controlled conditions, it should also be noted that there are several phenomena under the aegis of the orthodox sciences that do not submit to the requirement of repeatability. Meteors, eclipses, lightning flashes, and the northern lights are transitory, sporadic phenomena that are not under the control of any human agency and that cannot be repeated at the will of any investigator.

For the stern and rigid skeptic who demands such proof of psychical research as that offered by those scientists who can present a mathematical formula or a chemical distillation, there will be little forthcoming. But there are many areas in conventional sciences where such certitude cannot be attained. There is the entire area of theoretical physics and conjectures about outer space. How much of astronomy can provide tangible proof of its claims? And what of psychology, biology, and sociology? Who can ever accurately predict anything with certainty when living creatures are involved?

While no one has captured a human soul and kept it in a test tube for laboratory analysis, some serious researchers feel that the reality of the invisible human spirit is demonstrated to us every day. For example, when we speak with people, we are looking at their exteriors—their clothing, their skin, their hair—but the actual personalities to whom we are speaking remain invisible to us.

To the psychic sensitive, the mediumistically talented, that invisible, essential stuff of personality can survive without a physical brain and body. And the paranormally gifted authors of *The Murder of Marilyn Monroe* are convinced that they made contact with the Essential Self of the legendary actress. The kind of proof that they are able to offer more nearly resembles that of the legal proof acceptable in the courtroom. They present fact after fact that would seem not to have been known by anyone other than Marilyn Monroe or someone very close to her.

And the authors of this book are by no means the only ones who have encountered the restless spirit of Marilyn Monroe. Bob Slatzer, whose lengthy relationship with Marilyn led to their brief marriage in 1952, told my wife Sherry and me that he had been involved in an experiment that had actually manifested a full materialization of the spirit of the actress.

Informed by a psychic sensitive that an eleven-year cycle had passed which would make the evening of August 4, 1973, astrologically identical to the night when Marilyn died, Slatzer said that about 12:15 A.M., just outside the actress's house, a "terrific wind" suddenly began to blow with almost hurricane force. Then, from out of nowhere, the spirit of Marilyn Monroe appeared:

"She had on white slacks with a little black-and-white, splash-pattern top, little white loafers, and I could see a shock of blond hair. She started walking toward the car. I had goose bumps all over!" Bob told us.

"All of a sudden, she veered off to the left where there had once been a big tree. She just stood there, almost as if she were made of cardboard, but the figure was highly recognizable as Marilyn."

The ghostly figure moved down the street and walked through a couple of small drainage ditches before she vanished into thin air. Slatzer noticed that while his shoes left imprints on the concrete from the water in the ditches, the spirit of Marilyn Monroe had left none.

Interestingly, while Sherry and I were gathering information for our book *Hollywood and the Supernatural*, we also acquired information from the spirit world that protested the official pronouncement that Marilyn Monroe had committed suicide.

In 1982, on the twentieth anniversary of Marilyn Monroe's death, the renowned psychic sensitive Clarisa Bernhardt stood in the bedroom in which the screen's reigning love goddess had made her transition to the spirit world. As she watched, a small mass of swirling mist in a corner of the room assumed the features of Marilyn. At once, Clarisa told us, the spirit complained of having crossed over before her time.

Later, as Clarisa walked in the garden that had once been such a joy to the actress, her spirit appeared to Clarisa and revealed a number of Marilyn's past lives. "She had been an Aztec maiden sacrificed to the gods. She had been a sacrifice then—and in her most recent life on earth," Clarisa said. "It seemed so very important to Marilyn that her fans know that she did not commit suicide."

In a letter by Edward Wagenknecht which was published in *Films in Review* shortly after Marilyn

Monroe's death, the author stated: "If it is sentimental to ask for justice in death to a girl who never received it while she was alive, then I am glad to plead guilty."

We have before us in *The Murder of Marilyn Monroe* an extremely moving account that seeks to make us understand once and for all that Marilyn Monroe did not commit suicide, that she was murdered. Whether or not the information truly issues from the surviving spirit of the legendary actress must remain a question to be answered according to the convictions of each individual reader. Ponder the source as you feel you must, but I urge you to read this account of a remarkable spiritual adventure with an attitude of openness. You just may hear a soul crying out for justice.

—Brad Steiger
Phoenix, Arizona

Preface

"I want my fans to know that I did not kill myself, and I did not take all the pills I was supposed to that day. In fact, I was trying to clean up my act with the help of my analyst. My close friends were first threatened, and then convinced, to help lay plans for me to be killed. They were convinced that my death would be good for the country and good for the fate of our Party. I was eliminated by those who I loved and adored. I gave to a President all of my body and my very little brain. I gave to his brother all of this plus the little girl in me. I thought he loved me as 'Norma Jean' and not 'Marilyn.' And with the law that binds my spirit, I was given permission to whisper in your ear all that I know and all that I can remember. We all died the same fate. But I want to thank you for taking the time to listen and for caring and feeling. I have no other way of saying . . . Thank you."

—Statement given on July 16, 1990,
by the spirit of
Marilyn Monroe

THE MURDER OF
MARILYN MONROE

CHAPTER I

THE AUTHORS

My fascination with life-after-death theories began in the 1950's—with the emergence of the past-life regressions of Bridie Murphy. I became an avid reader of books on reincarnation, channeling, and other ghostly phenomena. At about the same time, I became a devoted fan of Marilyn Monroe's. I have always felt an affinity for Marilyn and have had her picture hanging in my study for years. How could I know where these two seemingly unrelated but continuing interests would eventually take me!

In 1975, I attended a lecture by Dr. Elisabeth Kübler-Ross, and I was convinced, after listening to her experiences with terminally ill patients, that we do possess a soul or spirit that leaves us at the moment of death. I have continued to learn through reading, meditation, and attending spiritualist classes.

I have been actively involved with the psychic community in my area for the last four years and became associated with Leonore Canevari in April 1987. Since that time, we have worked together on several projects involving contact with spirits.

I want the reader to know that much of the information we received during the course of developing this book was very painful for me to accept. It was bone-chilling and emotionally distressing to hear Marilyn's spirit describe how she was brutally and cold-bloodedly murdered while people she knew and trusted refused to interfere on her behalf.

To further compound my dismay, John F. Kennedy was the first President I campaigned for and voted for, and I have been a loyal supporter and defender of the Kennedy family since 1960. However, feelings aside, we were somehow selected by a higher power to receive these facts and share them with all who are interested.

This is my first attempt at writing, although through the years whenever I had a psychic reading done, the reader would always see me as a writer and encourage me in that direction. So, finally the course has become clear. As one of our spirit contacts explained: all things are planned ahead, and now we are all at the right time and the right place . . .

—Jeanette van Wyhe
—1990

I have been interested in psychic phenomena all of my life. For the past ten years I have believed that there is life after death and life before life. I have read a great deal about it through the years. I have also studied varied religions and found many common threads pertaining to their "life after death" beliefs and funeral practices.

The first entity I actually had direct contact with (two years ago) was a presence in my home, the ghost of a previous owner. I was skeptical at first of the information flooding in from her on the Ouija board. This woman was totally unknown to the seance group gathered in my home and known only by her last name to me. Later, in researching the factual information received, I found it to be verifiable in city and county records. Since that time I have had numerous encounters with various entities. The vast majority of information received from them has been verifiable.

At this time, there is no doubt in my mind that life after death does occur and that we on this earth are able to have contact with spirits in other worlds.

In the past ten years I have taken my personal growth very seriously. Much of my time and energy has been devoted to introspection, meditation, work with crystals and their healing properties, spiritual growth, and the kind of exploration that has generated this book.

I might add that to date, the task of gathering the information for this book has been one of the most interesting experiences I've ever had. From the beginning this project seemed to have a life of its own. I never knew where we were headed or what information would come from the interesting spirit friends we have made.

—Christian Dimas
—1990

My interest in psychic phenomena started at the age of seven or eight. I remember buying my first book about ghosts in the first grade at a book fair that took place in my school's cafeteria. Since then I have done much reading on the subject, and I never miss a movie or television program about ghosts, life after death, and other similar topics.

I have felt and seen a presence in my own home. About a year after seeing this entity, we made contact with it with the help of a Ouija board. This entity turned out to be a previous owner of the house. All the information she gave to us, when later researched, turned out to be factual.

I often have dreams that come true. Also, some of my dreams have held messages that were very significant in my life. However, I never dreamed that I would become involved with a project as fas-

cinating as the occurrences that have led to this
book.

—Rachel Dimas
—1990

My earliest recollection of the bizarre and unusual
would have to be at the tender age of about six. My
childhood, in many ways, was very much the same as
all the other kids on my block in Brooklyn, New York.
Outdoor play always consumed most of our vigor even
through the cold wintery seasons and the hot, very hu-
mid days of summer. The streets and the front stairs,
commonly known as the stoops, released us from the
confines of the small, sometimes overcrowded apartments where most of us lived.

Since our neighborhood was about 95 percent Italian, our apartments had a noticeable ethnic overtone.
Elk horns wrapped in strips of red material were clearly
visible above the entrance doors along with red cornas,
similar to goat horns, in all sizes to bring good luck and
break the evil eye which was called *malocchio*.

Priests carrying holy water were always visible on Fri-
days if a new neighbor had moved in. The holy water,
along with small fish provided by the tenant, was thrust
into the corners of each room to bring good luck,

peace, abundance, and good health to the new family. Oddly enough, a fishy scent never remained because the priests flushed the fish down the toilets before leaving.

My own apartment also had all of these ethnic touches, but there were other objects that seemed to set it aside from the other dwellings. Our hallways were filled with bookcases crammed with what were considered by some as unusual books. These early editions were steeped in the philosophies of the occult, texts transcribed from ancient Egyptian manuscripts, life after death and spiritualism, which was a subject that was taboo in those days. Oddly enough, spiritualists' message services were swamped by the very same people who were afraid to divulge their interest in this subject. There was one object in our apartment that attracted me the most, an eleven-inch crystal ball which seemed to give off an eerie iridescent glow that stimulated my young mind to search for the unknown mysteries of life.

Still implanted in my thoughts were the weekend, late-night gatherings at my grandmother's home. In that rather large dining-room area, family and friends assembled to tap into our passed-on relatives who directed them to lost, sought-after personal items and foretold of upcoming events. On one very momentous evening I witnessed a three-or-four-foot rising of what was called a three-legged table. During these unusual occurrences, I was supposed to be well into sleep instead of peering through the openings in the darkened stair railing which seemed to tower over these paranormal experiences.

In looking back to those earlier years, I find it impossible to forget my mother's stories about her spiritualist classes in the late 1920's. The most unforgettable story was her account of the students involved in these lessons. She estimated that half of her class was composed of clergymen. I guess this was not completely unusual, because our Catholic churches (especially the parishes in Italian communities which had Italian-born pastors, priests, and nuns) accepted the possibilities of saintly statues moving in glass domes, messages given during dream states, and ghostly visitations from dead relatives. In later years, I could not understand the dioceses' condemnation of such events until I heard a talk on the subject of Italian-American customs. The speaker pointed out that the Italian-American Catholic is quite different from any other group of Catholics because of the priority given to their ethnic customs. So, after giving this great thought, I came to the conclusion that I was truly fortunate to have a mother and a family that instilled in me at an early age the importance of having an open mind toward life, death, and universal law.

Shortly after my eighth birthday, I had my first encounter with a ghost. Whenever I slept at my grandmother's house, an elderly man visited me. He entered through a wall in the bedroom, sat in a chair for a while, and then exited the same way. To be sure that I wasn't hallucinating, my relatives encouraged my mother to take me to our family doctor who concluded that I was having a nervous breakdown at this early age. It wasn't until both my mother and grandmother saw this same elderly gentleman in that room did I get to stop the medicine and doctor's appointments.

After much badgering on my part, and soon after

this episode, my mother reluctantly agreed to include me in her Ouija board contacts. I shall never forget the excitement of my first response message.

Through the years, I have received a variety of messages from an assortment of passed-on souls. There were many times when some messages did not make too much sense, depending on the entity we were making contact with. One of the more memorable communications was from Carmen Miranda, a song-and-dance lady of the 1940's. She was my first spirit to question the facts surrounding her death. We accepted her message, but my mother did not feel that she was in a position to do anything about this disclosure.

The most disturbing message I ever received was a prediction involving a man that the entity insisted was my boss at work. The initials given me were not my boss's, so we wrote the information down and filed it with some of the more unusual messages received on the Ouija board. I did not think about it anymore until my new boss of about three weeks was killed in a tragic airline crash. That day, both my mother and I headed for our Ouija file which revealed my present boss's initials, date of death, name of airline destination, and time.

From my teen years through my twenties, I had many interests and belonged to many social and community organizations, but I was never able to dismiss an inner voice that kept nagging at me to return to my studies of the paranormal. I reluctantly consented to do the Ouija board with a number of people who had heard that I worked with the board. At that time in my life, I felt that I was still in the studying stage and was reluctant to have people's problems at my fingertips.

Going back to a day in the late sixties, I did, however, involve myself with a police department case. I did this more for concern over the dead woman's family than for my own personal psychic development. The case involved a brutal shooting of a lady. I did the Ouija board with police department personnel, and we came up with the name of the perpetrator and a reason for the killing. The case was never resolved due to lack of material evidence for prosecution.

In the sixties, I was exposed to my first encounter with practicing spiritualists whose transmediumship abilities were astounding. I joined a group which tapped into incidents involving hauntings, mysterious occurrences, and scores of other unexplained phenomena. At the time of my first exposure to an entity, I concluded that my field of study would definitely revolve around ghost contact.

I could not then and cannot now accept the theory that ghost communications are evil. In almost all of my lectures, I include remarks on this subject. I try to rationally approach this theory with the hope that my audience does not see a devilish being around each corner. I have always felt that a good practicing psychic or medium could differentiate between good and bad spirits just as we encounter good and bad humans during the course of life. I will not submit to a theory that the souls of our friends and family are being used and manipulated by the little man with two horns. I feel that God, who is all good, made possible the visitations of saints and dreams filled with messages and revelations; therefore He must be a positive force to be reckoned with.

My studies to become a spiritualist moved rather

41

slowly, I thought. I felt I was not progressing the way I should have been. My instructor told me I was too anxious and trying too hard. With time and patience I began to feel more comfortable with my accomplishments and my abilities of visualization during my meditation.

In the early 1980's, I explored the philosophies and the teachings of the metaphysical churches, and there I found the inner peace I needed to find the hidden universal power we all have buried within ourselves. My first actual visualization during meditation came at a metaphysical church service in New York. As I sat in deep meditation, I felt the presence of someone standing beside me. As I opened my eyes, I saw a rather lovely girl dressed in a shabby, cream-colored bridal gown. The sun glowing through the church window seemed to enhance her lovely brown hair, which was clearly visible under a limp, lacy veil topped by a garland of small white flowers. What seemed to startle me the most was the dog she had with her. The large animal proceeded to lick my left leg, which was festered from an ongoing, nasty rash. As I sat there I could actually feel the wetness of the dog's coarse tongue against my leg. The lady and her pet seemed to leave almost as quickly as they appeared.

As soon as the service ended, I rushed over to the minister to tell her of this startling incident. She drew me aside and told me that I was not the only one in her congregation who reported seeing such a bride walking with a dog. Before that day ended, the rash on my left leg showed improvement. By the next day, the festered area was gone, and the rash just seemed to disappear.

Shortly after I returned to California, the minister in

New York called to tell me that her members had decided to bring a spiritualist group into the church building to see if they could make a contact with an entity. Without telling the spiritualists anything about the ghost, they left them alone in the building for almost an hour. The group made contact with a lady who represented herself to them as a bride. She claimed to have been married in that building many years ago. In that same building, she was cast out of the congregation because they accused her of infidelity. She died alone with her dog after being forbidden to see her husband and child. She appeared as a bride in that structure because she said, "That was my happiest moment." The spiritualists told her that the sin she committed was truly forgiven and that if she returned to her burial place (which was an old paupers' cemetery) she would eventually reunite with her loved ones. As of that day the bride and her dog were never seen again.

From this time on, my meditations seemed easier, and I found that I was able to go deeper into meditation at will and just as quickly dismiss my meditative state. I continued to work in the paranormal, especially in the area of reincarnation because I found that many entities divulged some of the concepts of reincarnation. This philosophy seemed to answer some of the questions of why at times we are unable to contact certain spirits.

Like the millions of people involved in the field of metaphysics, reincarnation, and the paranormal, one finds that commitment to these studies brings about an inner perception of people's emotional turmoil. Such was the case a short time ago when a lady in my neighborhood was unable to find her kindergarten-aged son. He inadvertently strayed from his front lawn during the earlier part of the day while the older children were still at school. One of the family members who was quite upset came to my door to find out if I had seen the boy during the day. A scene that included this boy flashed through my mind. I visualized the boy seated on the floor inside a home. He was playing with an older boy, and there were toys piled in front of them.

I told the family member to knock on every door on the block. I was sure that he was in one of those homes. "There aren't any kids at home now, they're all still at school," the relative replied. I finally convinced him to do as I suggested, and within a short time they found the boy at a neighbor's home playing on the floor with an older boy who was home from school due to an illness. They found them in the neighbor's living room immersed in a pile of toys.

I tried to continue my meditative states even though at times it seemed too time-consuming. I also tried to collaborate with psychics whose area of expertise was ghost contact. In California I continued to work with various people in our organization and found that our abilities to make verbal contacts with spirits while in an altered state of mind were vastly improving. We noticed that there seemed to be a pattern of similar events surrounding the background of the ghosts. These contacts were made in both private and public buildings where there were numerous reports of ghost sightings and abnormal phenomena.

We experienced abnormal activity in old courthouses and restaurants which had a long history of traumatic events. The pattern we were establishing seemed to involve historical murders which had been recorded incorrectly in the history of that town or county. There seemed to also be an injustice done to all these entities who were returning to see to it that the records be corrected. Through the perseverance of our fact-finding committees and news reporters who took on the tedious job of researching old records and files, we found that we were changing some of the recorded facts in many criminal cases.

This brings me to our current group, which seems to be channeling with unusual success. Our group of psychics are uncovering great amounts of factual material pertaining to a questionable death. A death that the world will not let die.

One of the entities who seemed to play a very important part in this complex death stated to us: "There are reasons for information to come out at certain times. You are at the right time and right place . . ." So, in other words it is time for us to know this.

—Leonore (Lee) Canevari
—1990

CHAPTER II

THE WORLD OF THE PSYCHIC

For those readers who are not familiar with the field of the paranormal, we thought it would be helpful to explore the work of psychics. This should provide a better understanding of the communications and disclosures that were given us beginning in April 1990 and ending December 1, 1990.

The world of the psychic is one of the most misunderstood and yet one of the most intriguing disciplines in the world. Psychics, channelers, and mediums can trace their practices and beliefs back to the early prophets and mystics who searched the stars and heavens for answers to life, death, and universal law. Throughout history, mankind has documented predictions from revelations, written mystical literature, and told of supernatural experiences, which leads us to believe that there has been a continuous search for answers to our existence.

All human beings, to different degrees, think about the end of their lives. If we can feel comfortable with the theory that Man has a soul which separates from the physical body at the time of death, then we must ask what happens to this separated soul. Unfortunately, psychics tend to be grouped into one category, when, in actuality, this field is extremely diversified. The one common bond that links them would have to be the fact that they are open-minded students studying and exploring universal law.

A psychic does not only foretell the future. There are psychics who work in the areas of physical and mental healing. Some dwell in the realm of past lives in order to bring about an insight into one's own psychological outlook. Some give psychic messages through automatic writing, others reveal their psychic messages through painting and drawing. This field includes multiple areas of expertise such as work with crystals, card reading, palmistry, numerology, and precognition. Many psychics work through a spirit guide. The ability to communicate with their personal spirit guide usually takes an enormous amount of time and study.

This brings us to the psychics whose spiritualist studies enable them to communicate with passed-on souls. This type of psychic ability is rarely encountered. Most assuredly it is the least understood because of the subjective nature of the communion with those who have died. The basic conviction of the spiritualist is that the soul and its characteristics survive after death.

In an altered state of mind (a meditative or trance state), spirit communication can be done in a variety of ways. Some psychics, with the reinforcement of their spirit guides, speak directly to a spirit and can visualize a scene or scenes involving the entity. Others are given messages through their spirit guide. This type of psychic usually does not talk directly to the entity. Less often, a psychic allows a spirit to speak through them, a process referred to as trance channeling. Spirit communication can also be accomplished by the use of a Ouija board, a three-legged table, and by automatic writing.

Some entities need permission from a higher source in order to initiate or respond to a request for contact. Evidently souls can materialize, have verbal contact, and otherwise communicate with those on our plane. In reference to communications, one particular spirit may act as a representative or ambassador with the purpose of setting up a line of communication. Spirits who have evidently received permission to make contact also seem to be able to summon other passed-on entities who have pertinent information relating to an event.

The spiritualists who deal with passed-on souls often find themselves in the position of having to produce positive proof of their information. A spiritualist is compelled to interrogate an entity vigorously in order to secure facts that will convince society of the existence of ghost communication. It is unfortunate that psychics are sometimes judged on singular incidents and are not allowed to be incorrect on any one point. It is generally agreed that spirit contact and psychic readings can average about an 80 percent accuracy rate. We cannot say why it is not always 100 percent. Quite the contrary, when those in accepted, structured religions falter, they do so without having their religious philosophies questioned.

On the other end of the spectrum, there are a small

number of individuals who are attracted by the occult and choose to dabble in the black arts, sometimes known as satanic worship. In our opinion, these people sometimes involve themselves in evil practices because they are of that mentality. The mystique of a powerful demon fascinates them.

After a number of previous experiences with "ghost hauntings" we feel confident that we have established a certain pattern of spirit contact and communication. Our present group received messages through the Ouija board, visualizations, and direct contact including visual display of past events. This book brings to life our fascinating spirit contacts made with one of the most famous personalities of our century.

These contacts were made by entering into an altered state of mind or what would be commonly referred to as a deep, meditative state. The depth of meditation largely depended upon each individual. In order to bring about a oneness with a passed-on spirit or a series of events, we had to first physically and mentally relax, removing ourselves from our material surroundings and projecting our thoughts into pertinent scenes.

Our original communication with Marilyn Monroe was quite unexpected and startling, as we reveal in Chapter III. She kept her promise to connect us with the entities who were directly involved with her life and death. This fascinating lady shared with us some of her most intimate moments, along with the unnerving and diabolical scenes of her death. As a result of these contacts, our group of psychics endured both physical and mental fatigue. We experienced depression, anxiety, and unusual remorse each time she shared segments of her murder. We also experienced stomach pain, light-headedness, and numbness in the hands and feet during contact along with other related discomforts. Our sleep patterns were interrupted by dreams of this entity, and we finally came to the conclusion that our physical pain seemed to relate to the pain she experienced just before her passing.

Twice during the contact sessions, the spirit of Marilyn entered into one of our bodies, giving us a deeper insight into her feelings and personality. One of our more traumatic occurrences happened when one of the psychics awoke during the night experiencing the dying process. But through all of this, we tolerated these uncomfortable sessions. We laughed when she was witty and cried when she sobbed. At times, we found her clever and at times very naive, but we always found her to be a loving soul, seeking only to be loved in return. She was an earthbound entity driven by the need to have the story of her death told.

On February 18, 1991, we bid farewell to Marilyn and the group of entities who helped tell her story. They were dismissed with the hope that they would find peace and a release from the pain of hiding the truth. We promised our spirit friends that we would attempt to fulfill their wish to have the events of Marilyn's tragic death disclosed.

We believe we have freed Marilyn's earthbound spirit, but in our memory this lovely lady will always be with us until the day we ourselves leave this world.

CHAPTER III

BIRDIE WOOD INTRODUCES MARILYN MONROE

The members of the Association for Paranormal Investigation had planned to enjoy a spring break from the group's calendar, filled with encounters with passed-on souls, spirits who seemed to have the desire to be heard and a need to communicate. After spending a number of fall and winter evenings in cold, dark attics and creaky old historical buildings, we looked forward to a steady diet of communication with the living.

Spring seems to arouse feelings of new life and a rebirth of the earth. This enchanting season also brings lovely mornings and days where one feels the urge to throw open the windows to release musty smells that accumulate during California's cold winters. Ghost hauntings of spirits who manifest in human form toss objects, appear in mirrors, and peer around darkened stairwells were the furthest things from the minds of these investigators.

Nevertheless, in March of 1990, one of the psychics in this paranormal association received a request to check out a neighbor's home. The homeowner had the distinct feeling that she had an uninvited guest— namely, a ghost being. She also experienced the urge to write out the name of Marilyn Monroe every time she sat down to make out her bills, shopping lists, etc. The thought of starting another possible investigation with all the work involving group contact, the gathering of information, and then the checking of facts did not generate too much enthusiasm among the psychics, so they "sat on it" for a while with the hope that the disturbance would go away.

Go away it would not! So, on April 19, 1990, the investigation began. The contact was made on the Ouija board, and the following information was received:

> My name is Birdie Wood.

Q: Is that Bertha Wood?

BW: No, Birdie.

Q: What area do you come from?

BW: Minkler area.

Q: California?

BW: Yes.

Q: Parents' names?

BW: Robert Wood; mother, Emmye.

Q: Robert and Emilie?

BW: Just called her Emmye Heydcliffe Wood.

Q: Is Heydcliffe your mother's maiden name?

BW: Yes.

Q: Do you know the type of information we need to identify you?

BW: Yes, I'm smart and very pretty. My mother came from near San Francisco. My father came from the middle of the country.

Q: Do you mean the Midwest?

BW: Yes. My grandmother and grandfather are here also.

Q: Where? Do you mean buried?

BW: Yes, in Minkler area. Died in late 1800's.

Q: What were their names?

BW: James and Elizabeth.

Q: Can we go to their graves?

BW: Of course!

Q: What was your father's occupation?

BW: Sheep, fruit grower. He was real strict, but I was a little on the wild side. He had to punish me quite often. He was a political person.

Q: Birdie, why are you in these people's house? What is it you want?

BW: I like this house and the people in it. I know they were open-minded about spirits and would be able to get all of you together to have a seance.

Q: Why do you want a seance? We are talking to you right now on the Ouija board.

BW: More than the Ouija will be needed. I will talk to you again.

Soon after this communication, we went to the Fresno County Library. In a book entitled *History of Fresno County California* by Paul E. Vandor[1], we found a Robert M. Wood who was married to an Emmye Heydcliffe. They had one child, a daughter named Birdie Wood. Emmye was from San Francisco. The Woods resided in the Sanger-Minkler-Reedley area of California. Mr. Wood was in both the sheep and vineyard business, and was very active in politics.

Mr. Wood's parents were named Elizabeth and

James. They indeed came from a midwestern state: Iowa. In the cemetery listings of Fresno County, California, dated October 1988, we found the listing of Elizabeth Wood, who died on February 8, 1898, and James Wood who passed away on December 9, 1873. They are both buried at the old Sanger cemetery near Sanger, California.

According to the California Death Index, Birdie Wood's father, Robert M. Wood, died on September 29, 1945, in Fresno County. Her mother, Emmie (also spelled Emmye), died on September 6, 1950, in San Diego County. It appears that the information that our entity gave us is verifiably accurate, and we concluded that we were in contact with the spirit of Birdie Wood.

We were able to locate an old friend of Birdie who still resides in Sanger, California. He told us that she traveled to many countries and was a fun-loving, witty, lovely-looking lady who enjoyed life to the fullest. Information received from a former neighbor of Birdie's indicated that she married Joe Cline, her father's chauffeur. Joe was reported to have been a pilot prior to World War II, and at its onset, he became a naval air officer stationed in San Diego, California. At that time, Joe and Birdie lived in the Coronado and Chula Vista area of San Diego County. Their marriage did not produce any children, and it was said that they both had a very social lifestyle, entertaining many officers from the air station. Their affluent style of living was largely due to Birdie's inheritance and the exceptional education she had received in private schools. During our encounters with the spirit that gave her name as Birdie

Wood, we neglected to obtain her exact birth and death dates.

Later, in compiling this book, we found that we were unable to find a birth record of Birdie from the County of Fresno. According to the *California Roster*—Directory of State Services of the State of California—the city of Sanger in which the Woods resided did not incorporate until May 25, 1911, after Birdie's birth. Also, according to a Fresno librarian, prior to 1905, the State of California did not require the recording of births. According to information we received from an acquaintance of Birdie's, she died in 1979 as B. W. Cline, living in Chula Vista, California, until she reached her nineties.

The homeowner continued to have the urge to write out the name of Marilyn Monroe. So, on June 8, 1990, when we had our second contact with Birdie Wood, our first question to Birdie was why this lady felt that her hand is being manipulated to write out the name of this legendary movie queen.

Q: Are you in some way responsible for this?

BW: Yes.

Q: Why? What does Marilyn Monroe have to do with you?

BW: I did it to attract attention. Marilyn needs to communicate with someone.

Q: Birdie, can we talk to Marilyn Monroe? Could you contact her so that she can talk to us?

BW: I will try for you. Birdie Wood is a friend. Man with higher number, I can find out. Hang around. I'll try, stay. Number 1890 to place her here. We

> must be still because [she is] away from here, but
> she is trying to make contact.

During our research after this communication, we found in Anthony Summers's book, *Goddess*[2], the number 1890 is coincidentally part of the telephone number to Marilyn's personal phone at her Brentwood, California, home.

This June 8 session became the first in a series of contacts we had with what we believe to be the spirit of Marilyn Monroe. We continued our contacts with Marilyn, each time giving the number 1890 until we reached such an in-depth rapport with her that the number was no longer needed. A meditation and a slightly altered state of mind was all that was needed to bring about the grotesque events of her death.

On July 2, 1990, we had the first visualization of both Birdie and Marilyn Monroe together. In this visualization, Birdie was seen with her arms crossed, walking around our chairs, and it was with a mocking feeling like, "I can have fun if I want to!"

Birdie was seen wearing a long dark skirt with a ruffle at the bottom. Her blouse was a cream-colored, soft, satiny fabric which was gathered around the waist. She was a little on the chunky side, and her hair was pulled up on top of her head. It was loosely bound together, showing ringlets. Her face glowed like a cameo. She grinned at us as if to say, "Oh, boy, look at this!" It was felt that she was having fun with us.

We wanted her to stop walking around, and we asked her if she knew why we were there. "Yes," she replied as she nodded her head. She looked to her left as she stood in front of the group. It was almost as if she expected someone to come walking out. We then concentrated on Marilyn, and Birdie went to a far corner and sat down as an apparition of Marilyn Monroe entered the area.

After a question-and-answer session with the spirit identifying itself as Marilyn Monroe (included in Chapter V), Marilyn walked over to Birdie Wood, who was still seated. She bent over and put her arms around Birdie. There was a distinct feeling of affection between the two, for it was evident that without Birdie Wood, Marilyn would not be able to communicate the story of the night of her death. As another entity states in Chapter VI, Birdie is indeed the ambassador.

The group reflected upon how incredible it was that we might actually be in contact with the spirit of Marilyn Monroe. To assure ourselves that we did have communication with *her*, we proceeded to ask a series of questions designed to yield personal, verifiable information.

Q: So, you know that we have some questions for you.

MM: Yes.

Q: Do you want to get started, or do you want to tell us something?

MM: Hi, and I must tell you that some things are clear to me and some are not. I was born June 1, 1926. I was born in L.A. I died August 4, 1962. My mother's name was Gladys. My father's name was Mortenson. My mother didn't even know who my father was. I got Monroe from my mother's maiden name. I got the name Marilyn because my man, a picture man, liked it. It reminded him of someone. I married James Doughtery in 1942. I married DiMaggio in 1954 and Arthur Miller in 1956.

[Note: Verification was found for all of the above facts *except* the date of death, which is officially August 5, 1962.[3,4] Regarding the fact that her mother didn't know the identity of her father, there is speculation that he might be one of two men: Edward Mortenson or C. Stanley Gifford.[5]]

Q: It was rumored that you married Bob Slatzer. Did you actually marry him?
MM: Yes.
Q: Where did you get married?
MM: Mexico.
Q: In what city were you born?
MM: L.A. My foster sister's name was Connie Baker. I had lots of them [foster sisters]. Joe [DiMaggio] and I divorced because he couldn't take my depression. I tried to change, but I couldn't. I felt he was too good for me. I did some work with parachutes in a plant in L.A. [Verified[6]] It was a place that built planes. I put in folds and packed chutes. One didn't open, and they felt I wasn't responsible, so I painted. I dreamed too much.
Q: Everything in your house was white—your clothes and your rugs. Why was that important to you?
MM: I thought I was crazy, and I felt secure in a white place because that's where I belong. I liked everything white; it made me think of an insane asylum.
Q: You weren't really insane. You know that, don't you?
MM: Many people in my family are insane.
Q: That doesn't make you insane.

MM: If they didn't kill me, I probably would have wound up in an insane asylum.

Q: That's true, but that was because of the alcohol and drug use.

MM: I was trying, I was really trying.

Q: You sound as if you are in a lot of pain.

MM: Yeah.

Q: On June 17, 1990, we were given certain facts, such as the number 1890 for contacting you. We found out that it was the number of your personal telephone.[7] We also asked the color. Give us your full personal number, the number of your other phone, and the colors of your phones. Start with your personal phone number.

MM: GR 6-1890 [Verified as one of her phone numbers.[8]]

Q: What color was that phone, Marilyn?

MM: White.

Q: What's the number of the other phone?

MM: GR 2-4830 [Verified as one of her phone numbers.[9]]

Q: Now, what was the color of that phone?

MM: Pink.

Q: You called the Justice Department a number of times during your last days. What was that number?

MM: RE 7-8200.

[Note: This number was given to us by Marilyn again on November 19, 1990, as the number of the Justice Department which she used to call Bobby Kennedy. (This was verified.[10]]

Q: How is it that we are able to communicate with you?

MM: Call BW [Birdie Wood].

BW: Marilyn cannot talk unless with permission.

Q: Haven't others tried to contact Marilyn?

BW: Yes, but she didn't think they were sincere.

MM: They couldn't feel my pain and my problems.

Q: Is there anything you would like to tell us?

MM: Have a nice picture of me in the book.

Q: Do you have a favorite picture you would like in the book?

MM: Yeah, when I was real young, because I was getting bags under my eyes—too much drinking.

Q: How young? Before you dyed your hair?

MM: No, after.

Q: Did you not like the pictures when you had your hair brown?

MM: No, no!

Q: We need you to tell us something, we're a little lost. We need some help. You want us to do something or you wouldn't have contacted us. What is it you want us to do?

MM: I want the truth. I want it to come out that I did not kill myself. I don't want people to think badly of me.

CHAPTER IV

AUGUST 4, 1962

"A swirling light . . .
a distance away was my bed . . .
. . . fading . . .

I thought I was hallucinating until I was told differ-
ently. I was given the opportunity to see so many
things, so I could understand the reason for where I
thought I was. I was taken to a room with other people.
People looked like they wanted to, and that made them
happy. Without anyone saying or explaining anything,
we just knew certain things. I have done some bad
things, but I know I will, or can, have another chance."
—Statement given on June 15, 1990,
by the spirit of
Marilyn Monroe

This chapter consists of visualizations of scenes as
well as direct conversations with a spirit that identified

itself as Marilyn Monroe. In these visualizations, the events were seen as though one was a spectator looking into the back of a doll house. It was as if the back were removed, giving at times a clear view of what was happening in more than one room. The visualized scenes were similar to watching a movie. The following visualizations do not immediately answer all of the questions surrounding this event; however, the reader will find further details in subsequent chapters. On occasion, some question and answer information was incorporated into the visualizations in order to clarify events for the reader.

In our contacts with Marilyn, she was always seen wearing a white, tight-fitting, floor-length dress. There was an opening in the front and a crossed band up around the bust with thin straps. She had an unusual, penguinlike walk as though her skirt was very tight.

On the afternoon of August 4, 1962, at approximately 2:00 P.M., a black sedan pulls into the driveway facing the front entrance of Marilyn Monroe's Brentwood home. The two front doors of the sedan open first. The driver, a rather attractive man in his late twenties with sandy-colored hair, gets out of the car. He is wearing a white shirt and dark pants. Out of the other door emerges a tall, thin, well-built man in his early forties with medium-brown hair and light eyes, wearing an expensive blue-gray suit with a dark tie. He has a sinister quality about him which, when looking at him, makes one feel very uneasy. This particular individual has a noticeable protruding gum line which brands him as much as a scar or tatoo would. If one were engaged in a conversation with him, it would be difficult not to stare at this very dominant characteristic. According to psychic information given us, this person was identified as "Dave" (see sketch #1).

With an air of diplomacy and a look of determination on his face, a very recognizable Robert F. Kennedy steps out of the right rear door of the car. He is wearing a short, dark, zip-up jacket. As the three men approach the front entrance, the door immediately opens as if their arrival were anticipated. The driver, unsure of what he is supposed to do, stops at the door while Robert Kennedy and Dave enter the Monroe home. According to Marilyn Monroe, one of her friends opens the door for them, and, sensing that Marilyn is very overwrought, retreats to the bathroom and remains there until the men leave.

Once inside, Kennedy, followed by Dave, veers to the right and heads toward a door as if he knows exactly where he is going. Although the house is very quiet, there is a definite tenseness in the air, like the calm before the storm. Bobby and Dave enter Marilyn's bedroom, and Marilyn, who is lying on the bed, sits up as she sees them. Wearing a white satin top and matching bikini panties, Marilyn is sitting on the bed with her legs over the edge facing the door. Grinning, she watches Bobby pull up a chair. The chair is not in the best condition, and he's looking at it wondering if it will hold him. Bobby sits down and crosses his left leg over his right and skeptically looks down at the back and legs of the chair to insure himself of its stability. Dave is standing against the wall with his hands clasped together over his groin area in a typical bodyguard position.

At this point, the conversation between Bobby and

Marilyn seems to be of a friendly nature. Marilyn is relieved and glad to see him. Her earlier frustration has diminished. Marilyn is speaking to Bobby, but it is not clear what she is saying. However, he responds with such phrases as, "What! Are you crazy? What's wrong with you? What the hell is wrong? Have you gone crazy?"

On the floor beside her bed there is a messy pile of papers. Marilyn leans over and picks up a piece of paper. She attempts to hand this paper to Bobby, but it is grabbed by Dave, who quickly glances at it. The paper does not remain in Dave's hand long because Marilyn grabs it back and hands it to Bobby once again. Bobby opens the piece of paper, reads it, then studies it a minute. Now Dave acts disinterested. Bobby Kennedy is saying something like, "I don't know what I can do about this!" Marilyn then says, "Of course you can do something about it." Bobby takes the piece of paper with his right hand, opens his zippered jacket, and slides the note inside a pocket, saying something like, "Well, tell you what . . . I'll see what I can do about this. The problem with you is that you're too damned hysterical!" Marilyn replies, "I'm not hysterical."

The significance of this note is monumental. It may be the most central issue of Marilyn's murder. The note listed subjects she intended to reveal and discuss at a press conference that had been planned for Monday morning, which would have been Monday, August 6, 1962. According to Marilyn, included on the list of topics was her relationship with Bobby, the Bay of Pigs, Mob use, and Air Force strength (Bobby had talked about how weak the U.S. was).

A friend of Marilyn's, Jeanne Carmen, was interviewed on *The Reporters Special Edition* television program entitled "Marilyn—A Case for Murder."[1] According to Ms. Carmen, "She [Marilyn Monroe] was going to talk to the press the following day or on Monday and people might have been desperate." Also on *The Reporters* Marilyn's former husband, Bob Slatzer, said in reference to Marilyn Monroe, "She told me on Friday evening prior to her death, 'If Bobby don't call me, I'm going to call a press conference on Monday morning, and I am going to blow the lid off this whole damned thing!' "

On that same show, Krista Bradford stated, "Carmen and . . . John Danoff reported that Marilyn had told them that if Bobby Kennedy did not make a commitment to her, she would reveal her involvement with him and brother, John Kennedy. She had threatened to make the announcement on August 6, a day after she died." (August 5 was the legally recorded date of her death.)

Returning to the visualization, Marilyn Monroe is very upset and is becoming angry, as if something had set her off. Bobby is upset, too. He gets up from the chair, puts his back to her, and covers his mouth with his hand. He's choked up, upset, trying to hold back a burst of emotion. He's fighting tears. He is not facing Marilyn, and she says, "Look at me!" Bobby just stands there fooling with the zipper of his jacket. He doesn't want to look at her. Dave says to Marilyn in essence, "I think you need to relax—I think you had better lie down." He goes to the door, opens it, and someone hands him a glass of water. The person handing the water to Dave is not visible, but the distinct impression is that the need for water was anticipated. Bobby hasn't changed his position. He is just standing there looking at nothing. Dave takes the glass of water over to Marilyn, who then lies down with her head tilted up. She takes the pill that Dave gives her. According to Marilyn, the pill was purplish in color, and she thought that she had taken this type of pill before.

Bobby is very upset, as if he's doing something he doesn't want to do. He's very emotional and confused. He has an hysterical feeling that he cannot control. He turns sheepishly and starts to walk out. Dave puts his left hand on Bobby's right shoulder and says what sounds like, "Don't worry about it. I'll take care of it." And they walk out of the room.

Dave and Bobby leave Marilyn's room; Bobby Kennedy exits the house. Dave pauses for a moment to put his arm around and say a few words to an older lady. This gesture on Dave's part is to give support to this lady. As soon as the driver of the car sees Bobby coming out of the house, he quickly moves to open the door on the passenger's side for him. When Dave enters the automobile, they back out of the driveway.

Marilyn Monroe is lying on her bed. She turns over on her right side, reaches down, and picks up a piece of paper and a blue-and-white pen. She also grabs something else, which she puts under the paper and begins to write. She pauses to think. She is calmer now and continues writing. This was a letter to Peter Lawford. In it she told him, among other things, that "he would go down, too, even though he was a friend" and she "loved him like a brother." We learned from the spirit of Peter Lawford that Marilyn was trying to threaten him so that he would encourage Bobby to continue their relationship (see Chapter VI).

Marilyn rolls over again and reaches down into the clutter on the floor. She picks up a white envelope, puts the letter in it, and licks the back. This envelope remains in her left hand while the pen is lightly resting in her right. Marilyn is very relaxed, and there is the feeling that the whole room is spinning around and around. Marilyn tells us that her friend came out of the bathroom at this point, stopped at her bed, looked back, left the room, and then left the house. Marilyn senses that this was around 2:00 to 3:00 P.M., shortly after Dave and Bobby left.

As Marilyn lies back, her door opens, and the elderly woman comes in. Marilyn struggles to sit up, and the woman attempts to calm her. She takes the pen and envelope out of Marilyn's hands and looks back at her while leaving the room. As she closes the door behind her, Marilyn is stretched out on the bed, in a position resembling Christ on the cross.

There is no visualization of a clock, but the time is felt to be around 3:30 P.M. still in the afternoon of August 4, 1962. In another room, the elderly woman walks over to a small table and picks up the telephone. It is interpreted as a call to a doctor. As she is putting through this call, it seems as though she is becoming very upset. Her exact words are not clear. She paces back and forth and seems very nervous, as though she is waiting for something. Suddenly, she stops dead in her tracks and literally runs to the front door. The doctor is there. Marilyn stated that this was the first time the doctor came to her home that day but added that she called him twice. The first call was around 1:00 P.M. on that afternoon of August 4, 1962. She told him that she was scared, and he suggested she take a pill and calm down. The second call was soon after Bobby left when she told the doctor about the letter she had given Bobby explaining what she planned to do about him and his brother at the press conference. Again, the doctor told her to calm down and that he had to go someplace first but would come over to her house later.

Now at the Monroe home, the feeling is that the doctor is anxious and distraught. He wants to know what is going on. The elderly woman is very nervous and starts to cry. The doctor tries to get her to collect herself. She goes over to the table where she has the letter she took from Marilyn and hands it to the doctor. He rips open the envelope, looks at the letter, and puts it back down on the table. He is in a panic and doesn't know what to do. He reaches for the phone and completes a call. There are numerous phone calls made. However, we were unable to get a sense of to whom these calls were made.

Refocusing on Marilyn's room, there is a sensation of dizziness—a whirling feeling like in *The Wizard of Oz* when the house is spinning. Looking now into the driveway of Marilyn Monroe's home, there are blinking lights coming. It is an ambulance with red lettering on a round red light on top. As the elderly woman and the doctor run to the door to open it, the feeling is that the ambulance was expected. Two men rush in, and are escorted into Marilyn's bedroom. Marilyn is lying on the bed in the same position as last seen. The two ambulance men, one older, in his fifties, and one younger, have on light-colored jackets. They proceed to work in some manner on Marilyn's left arm, with motions similar to karate chops. Her head bobbles back and forth. She can see these men; she looks at them with her head still bobbling as if she's having some sort of seizure. Marilyn tells us the older man seemed to think that they would be able to arouse her at this point. Suddenly, Marilyn's bedroom door opens. Dave, who is alone, is back in the house. He enters Marilyn's room, looks around, walks over to her bed, and says something to the two ambulance men like, "Come out of here." He is ordering the men out.

The younger fellow stops immediately and walks toward the door while the older man doesn't seem to feel that he should be told what to do. So he keeps working on Marilyn's arm. Dave calmly says to him what sounds like, "I told you to come out. I'm in charge of this. Come out now!" The older man looks back and shakes his head in disgust as he leaves.

The main room of the house, which is not too far from Marilyn's bedroom, seems to be the center of activity during the remaining hours of the actress's life. The two ambulance men now seem deflated as they converse with Dave, the elderly woman, and the doctor. About five minutes pass, and the ambulance men finally turn around and let themselves out the front door. They pull out of the driveway and leave.

The elderly woman picks up the envelope intended for Peter Lawford, which had been placed back on the small table, and now gives it to Dave. He reads the note with a grin on his face. He shoves it back into the envelope, looks toward Marilyn's door, and walks in. She is still lying on the bed, and he casually throws the envelope onto her bed. Now there appears to be something written on the envelope which had been blank before.

The next series of events begins at approximately

5:00 P.M. on this afternoon of August 4, 1962. There are shadows in Marilyn's room, and the lamp on the floor is on even though light isn't needed yet. Back in the main room, Dave is present while the elderly woman and the doctor are talking. The doctor is very upset, and the feeling is that he is disoriented. The elderly woman does not seem as distraught, more contained. The doctor seems to say, "I can't do this." Dave pulls back his jacket and puts his hand in his pockets saying in essence, "You can do it. You are going to do it. That's enough out of you!"

The doorbell rings. Dave opens the door, and in the doorway there stand two people. One, later identified by Marilyn as "Jimmy" (see sketch #2), is a rather good-looking, ruddy-complexioned man who is very neatly dressed in a light blue suit and tie. He has light-brown hair which is slightly wavy. As he enters the house, it is noticed that he is carrying a small black bag. A middle-aged, tall, thin lady, whose name may be "Adele" (see sketch #3), is standing behind him. She is very astute-looking, like a schoolmarm. She is dressed in a navy-blue dress with white cuffs and a Peter Pan collar. Her stockings are light in color, and she is wearing dark, low-heeled shoes. Her dark hair is pulled back tightly into a bun which allows only her earlobes to show. Adele, whose hair is slightly streaked with gray at the temples, has noticeably high cheekbones which accent her nice-looking complexion. Her skin seems to be extremely tight and smooth. She is very plain and is not wearing much makeup. She is light-skinned, rather pale, in fact, and very thin.

Adele is in her early forties. She has a sharp nose, pointed chin, and almond-shaped dark eyes. Her eyes are cold and piercing. Her eyebrows are close together and look very even, as if she has worked with them. She is wearing a gold chain with a crucifix which has the unusual Celtic sunburst design. Adele, who is an articulate, competent woman, also appears to be very tense and sinister.

Dave tells Jimmy and Adele to come in, and he immediately draws them into a corner by the front door. Adele seems to be carrying the bulk of the conversation with Dave. As they converse, Dave is displaying a lot of hand motion, and the feeling is that he is trying to rationalize this situation and calmly make a decision. The impression received regarding this conversation is that Dave knows these two people, not as if they are good friends, but as if he has worked with them before in some capacity. He does not have to explain the reasons for this meeting as they are already aware of the situation. This threesome seems to be connected by a sinister common denominator.

As the conversation continues, it is briefly interrupted by Adele, who leaves to go into Marilyn Monroe's bedroom. Marilyn looks like she is in a deep sleep. Adele goes over to her and unties a ribbon of some kind which is bound around Marilyn's waist and slips her arm out of her white jacket. She proceeds to remove Marilyn's white panties and folds them neatly at the foot of the bed. Marilyn senses the removal of her clothes and becomes frightened. It is felt that she knows what is happening, so she lifts her head, bringing her chin into her chest as though she is trying to focus on her naked body. She immediately rolls over and reaches for the phone. Adele, very annoyed and indignant, pulls the phone out of Marilyn's hand and puts it back on the receiver. Marilyn says that when the phone was taken away from her, she was attempting to call Sam Giancana but never did get to contact him that day.

Realizing that Marilyn Monroe is still functioning, Adele turns around, leaves the room, and says something to the two men still in the corner. Jimmy now goes into Marilyn's room with his black bag. Adele follows him in, moves around to the other side of the bed, and holds Marilyn's left arm—the same arm the ambulance driver was hitting. Adele is putting considerable pressure on Marilyn's left arm right above the elbow. She is pushing down quite hard with one hand pressed on top of the other to prevent Marilyn from moving the arm. This is painful to Marilyn, and she squirms around.

Jimmy drops his small black bag onto the floor and reaches into it. He grabs and lifts Marilyn's right breast. As he puts something into the breast area, Marilyn Monroe lets out a cry. They know she is still alive and that she is crying because they hurt her. In reference to this action, we asked Marilyn if she was given an injection by this man. In trying to explain what she felt, Marilyn replied that it pinched and hurt, but she did not see what he was doing. "It hurt and it burned, and I felt like I had pressure on my chest. I couldn't breathe."

Both the man and the woman leave the room, slamming the door behind them. As they return to the main room Adele just stands there, and the doctor can't seem to contain himself; he walks around throwing his arms in the air. Shortly thereafter, Jimmy and Adele leave but not before being served a cup of coffee.

There is a passing of time in the visualization. The scenario picks up at a later time during the day when Dave, the elderly woman, and the doctor are still in the Monroe home. The doctor is in tears, but the elderly woman is now feeling cool and calm about these events. Dave is walking around the room, annoyed that the elderly woman and the doctor are butting into his plans. Dave walks over, sits himself in a chair, and picks up a newspaper. He leans back and reads the paper as if nothing is bothering him.

There is someone at the door. Dave puts the paper down and goes to the door. It is rather dark, and there is no outside light. Dave is talking to someone, raising his voice, saying what sounds like, "This is bullshit!" Two men come in, and it seems as though it is without Dave's permission. One of the men is an older man. He is wearing a long black coat and has a military haircut which is heavily streaked with gray. This man has rather large black eyes that seem to fit his oversized body. He is identified to us as "Tony" (see sketch #4). The younger man, identified as "Phil," also has dark hair, but it is exceptionally long for these early years of the 1960's. He has a noticeable scar on the left side of his chin (see sketch #5). Marilyn thinks she remembers him from a hotel party that she attended near the Eliot Hotel in Boston at which Peter Lawford was present.

There is an argument going on between Dave and these two men. They continue arguing with Dave even after they enter the house. Dave doesn't seem to be too happy as he informs them in essence, "I tell you what to do, you don't tell me what to do." As the argument continues, the doctor jumps out of his chair. He can't contain himself; he doesn't know what to do. He is absolutely going crazy. The elderly woman gets up and walks around telling him to calm down. He says something that sounds like, "This is ridiculous, I don't know right from wrong anymore!"

As the three men continue to argue, Tony tells Dave something to the effect of, "Hey, I don't give a damn what you say." The two men go to Marilyn's bedroom, open the door, and enter. Marilyn is only semiconscious but sees them walking toward her bed. As they approach, it is sensed that Marilyn is feeling a burst of reality as she is thinking to herself, "This is the last straw." She is extremely upset at this point, and she starts kicking her legs. Tony goes over to her and grabs her face, telling her to shut her mouth. He actually does the opposite as he opens her mouth and puts something from his pocket into it.

Pills are being put down her throat. He is trying to stick them into the back of her mouth. She gags and tries to spit them out. He is cursing at her and calling her a bitch. He pulls his hand back, and she is spitting. In fighting back, she evidently bit him, as blood is noticed on his finger.

There is a slight disagreement between the two men, and Tony tells Phil not to be "chicken-shit". Tony puts on a pair of cream-colored rubber gloves. The blood is visible in the glove. Phil, who is on Marilyn's left side, grabs her right arm while Marilyn is lying on her back and brings it under her body as he pulls her toward him. Tony grabs her left arm, and they turn her roughly onto her stomach. He then shoves something into her rectum. Marilyn felt "a burning sensation, many black moments, stomach eruptions, and a loss of control [urination]".

At this point, Marilyn is no longer struggling. She is feeling excruciating pain. She feels violated, and she knows she is going to die. There is nothing this woman can do. Lying there on her stomach, she gives up. According to Marilyn, her time of death is approximately 9:30 P.M., August 4, 1962.

The two men walk out of Marilyn's bedroom and casually look back. It is felt that they show no remorse for what they had just done. They do stop for just a minute but only to give Dave "the finger" as they turn and walk out of Marilyn Monroe's home. Dave makes his way back to Marilyn's room. He looks at her and leaves, locking the door behind him. He tries the knob to make sure it's locked. He leaves the house between 10:30 and 11:00 P.M. Marilyn Monroe is dead.

The elderly woman and the doctor find themselves alone once again. She is displaying some emotional distress as she asks something like, "What are we going to do?" He motions for her to come with him, and they go outside leaving the front door open. It is dark out as they go around to the back of the house. The doctor has something in his hand which he is banging against the wall. They re-enter the house, close the door, and sit down. According to Marilyn, they were having a "dry run" of what they would have to do later that evening. They wanted to make sure they had a clear passage to her window, the window that was to be used as an entrance to her room later that night.

Time passes, and during that time the phone keeps ringing; the elderly woman and the doctor take turns jumping up to answer it. The conversations are short. The doctor has a key in his hand and opens Marilyn's door. She follows him in. The doctor has bottles of pills in his hands, and he is spilling the pills on the floor. Marilyn claims that they then remove her from her bed. She holds her head and the doctor her legs. They place her on the living-room floor in order to change the sheets. When the bed was remade, they again carry her in the same way and place her back in the bed on her stomach.

The elderly woman puts the phone on the bed; the dial tone is audible. They leave the room, locking the door behind them. The doctor hands the key to her, which she puts in the pocket of her sweater.

Soon after, a blue-and-white ambulance arrives from a different company, and the men enter the house. (In questioning Marilyn about the ambulances, she claims that there were two ambulances and one coroner's car at her home from the afternoon of August 4 through the early hours of August 5.) The doctor talks to the drivers and leads them around to the backyard. The ambulance drivers climb through the unlocked window of Marilyn Monroe's room and unlock the door from the inside. The doctor and the elderly woman enter the room, and the doctor tells the ambulance men, "She must have died." One of the men listens for a heartbeat, not long, only for a second.

We asked Marilyn who had called this second ambulance. Her answer was that Dave called for it from Peter Lawford's Santa Monica beach house around 11:00 to 11:30 P.M. She also related that one of the ambulance drivers, who was rather "small and skinny," refused to take her body because she was already dead. According to Marilyn, the doctor panicked and quickly called Dave. Dave demanded to talk to this ambulance driver, and when he got on the phone, Dave told him that this was a "top security" matter. They had to take her out and to the hospital. Marilyn claimed that Dave said, "I'll make it worth your while." The ambulance driver was quick to respond to this order and did what he was told. In this part of the visualization, Marilyn was seen with no clothing on. They wrapped her in something dark, strapped her onto a gurney, and went out the door.

Marilyn is in the ambulance. More cars pull up, four in all. There is a man there with very curly, kinky hair. He is wearing glasses and has a rather large nose. He is backing his car into the driveway and is talking to the ambulance driver. Marilyn identified this man as Arthur Jacobs, her press agent, but could not identify the other man with him. [According to Summers in *Goddess*, Jacobs received the news of the death at approximately 11:00 P.M. while attending a concert and had left at once for Marilyn's house.[2]]

Marilyn tells us that Jacobs said to the ambulance drivers, "You can't take her out . . . you gotta put her back. She's dead." The drivers take her body out and wheel her back into the house. They are standing in the main room with the gurney, and they are all talking. The doctor is trying to answer everyone's questions. Marilyn remarked to us, "The whole thing is crazy." She continues, saying that the doctor runs back into the house, phones Dave, who says to the drivers, "I'm telling you take her out . . . this is a federal thing . . . you can't interfere."

This confusion continues for ten to fifteen minutes, and they finally decide to take her out again and put her back into the ambulance. They back up and pull out of the driveway. It is not clear where they were taking her this second time, perhaps to the hospital as suggested by Anthony Summers's book, *Goddess*. Summers quotes the late Walt Schaefer, the ambulance company chief, who said they took her to Santa Monica Hospital. However, according to Summers (p. 394), "Initial research at Santa Monica Hospital has borne no fruit."[3]

In the ambulance the men are arguing. The smaller man panicked and said, "It is insane, it's not worth the money. I'm taking this body back." They return and put Marilyn's body back inside the house.

Everyone is talking at the same time. An older man in the crowd has a badge though he's not wearing a uniform. He is trying to tell everyone to shut up and to talk one at a time! The house is full of people, but its owner, Marilyn Monroe, is gone.

Sketch #1

Sketch #2

Sketch #3

Sketch #4

Sketch #5

CHAPTER V

ACCORDING TO MARILYN . . .

In question-and-answer form, the spirit of Marilyn Monroe clarifies certain events in the previous chapter.

Q: What exactly do you want us to do? Do you want us to bring out the truth about your death?

MM: Yes. I knew there was danger in the time before I died, but the pills and my phobia stopped me from thinking rationally.

Q: What phobia are you talking about?

MM: Fear that people were following me, fear that people didn't like me, fear that people were staring at me.

According to Marilyn:

Friends around her for the last couple of days were supposed to keep her drugged. That is why she believes she was so disoriented. Even so, when Dave came in he thought she was too rational. He was supposed to call the shots on whether or not she was going to die—depending on how rational she was and if she was going to go through with the tattle-telling press conference. If she was drugged and "out of it," she would not be a threat to anyone at that time. But, if she was rational, her press conference was going to be a very real thing. So, when Dave saw her, he decided she had to die!

Several of Marilyn's friends were there within a two-day span, and Marilyn was encouraged to take pills because she seemed so nervous. Each of these friends had been visited individually and were told that this is what they had to do. They were told that it was necessary for Marilyn to die for the good of the country and for the fate of the political party. If they could keep her drugged, they wouldn't have to kill her.

MM: What do you want to know?

Q: Were you murdered?

MM: Yes.

Q: Why do you think they wanted to murder you?

MM: I told Peter that I missed my period and wasn't sure which one, Bobby or John, was the father. But, I told him that I would think about who I would blame depending on which one called first. I was unable to get out of my room earlier in the day because I heard voices in the house and the door was locked. I had no food and took pills when he [Peter Lawford] sounded like he didn't give a damn. He's a stool pigeon and took more drugs than I did. The boys needed to shut me up.

Q: Who?

MM: Kennedys. They knew many Mob boys that were kissing up to Bobby because of his position, and I told Bobby I would squeal and tell their wives

because I wanted them to squirm. They were using me, and John told me he would marry me.
[Bobby] was in love with me, too. Only used Ethel
for family. Bobby is a bastard.

Q: Did Rose Kennedy know?

MM: She never asked questions.

Q: Why were you making phone calls [on August 4]?
       Were you asking everyone for pills?[1]

MM: No, I was asking for help.

Q: Did you ask for pills that morning[2]?

MM: No.

Q: What kind of help did you call for?

MM: I wanted someone to come over because I was
       frightened.

Q: What else do you want to tell us? Anything more
       about Dave?

MM: He was back in the house all day. I knew he was
       there.

Q: Did he administer any kind of a drug to you?

MM: Yes.

Q: How did he do this?

MM: It was a pill.

Q: What time of day was this?

MM: About 2:30.

This pill was stronger than the ones she usually took.
She did not take many pills that day because she was
really trying to turn over a new leaf prior to all this. She
was really trying not to take too much medication. She
had taken one of her pills the night before, one when
she got up in the morning, and had a half a glass of
beer just before lunch. So, on August 4 she had the pill
she took and the pill Dave gave her.

Dave made the decision that Marilyn Monroe was to
die, and he started the process. He told the other peo-

ple about his decision over the phone but had already been instructed to go ahead if needed. J. Edgar Hoover himself called him to find out what was happening, and Dave told him what the situation was.

Q: How do you know this?
MM: I don't know, I just know it.
Q: Do you know who Dave called when he made this decision?
MM: It was a Washington call.
Q: Did John know about this decision?
MM: Yes.
Q: Bobby?
MM: Yes.
Q: Did John order this?
MM: He came to a decision, he didn't order it.
Q: Isn't that the same thing?
MM: Yes, because he had to meet with other people to discuss it. It wasn't his decision alone.
Q: Marilyn, did Bobby Kennedy have you killed?
MM: Mob and negotiation, but he gave permission to kill because Bobby promised . . . no interference.
Q: Are they [the Kennedys] still scared?
MM: Yeah, the bottom line is they're afraid of their family name.

MM: I saw Bobby Kennedy the day I died. He came to talk about 2:00 P.M. But I said I was "disgusted," and a man gave me something to sleep. I took the pill with a glass of water. Bobby left at 2:30 P.M. The pill made me tired.
Q: Was Bobby there at your *house* that day?
MM: Yeah.
Q: Did you argue? Was he angry?
MM: No, he wasn't really angry. Just frustrated, upset. He's a jerk.

Q: When he left, what did he say to you?
MM: Nothing. He wouldn't look at me.

Marilyn explained the letter she had written. There were *two* letters—the one that Bobby took and another one on the bed. The letter on the bed (in an envelope) was a letter to Peter Lawford. In it she told him that "he would go down, too, even though he was a friend and I loved him like a brother." She did not write his name on the envelope. Peter destroyed this letter when he went over to clean up.

Q: What was on the note Bobby took?
MM: It was a list of the things I intended to say at a press conference Monday morning.
Q: What was on the list?
MM: Our relationship, the Bay of Pigs, Mob use, combustion.
Q: What does "combustion" mean?
MM: Air Force strength—he talked a lot about how weak we were.
Q: Why were you going to disclose all these things to the press? Didn't you know you'd be in trouble?
MM: I thought I would be his wife; he never said no.
Q: Didn't you know you were dealing way over your head? Didn't they have Mob connections?
MM: So did I.
Q: Yours didn't do you any good though.
MM: I couldn't get to them in time.
Q: Who were you trying to call when the woman [Adele] took the phone out of your hand?
MM: Giancana. [Sam Giancana—head of the Chicago Mafia at that time.]
Q: Was he very upset over your death?
MM: Yes.

Q: Do you know whose child you were pregnant with?

MM: Bobby's.

Q: Were you really pregnant?

MM: I think so.

Q: How late were you?

MM: Two months.

Q: Why did you play around so much? Why couldn't you just stick to one relationship?

MM: They always loved me.

Q: What about your right breast? Do you know what was in that injection?

MM: Something to trigger the heart.

Q: Is there an important point we missed?

MM: Yes. Needle.

Q: We are going to hold up a picture; tell us if you recognize it? (We hold up sketch #1.)

MM: Yes. He was in the house the day I died.

Q: Does this picture look like him?

MM: Pretty much so.

Q: Do you have the name of this man?

MM: Dave.

Q: How do you know this man? What was he doing in your house?

MM: He was there with Bobby.

Q: We want to know this man's role. What was his job?

According to MM:

Dave was one of J. Edgar Hoover's men assigned to Bobby to make sure that Marilyn would be taken care of. When Dave came there he was already aware that if he decided to have her killed it could and would be done. The decision to have her dead that day was made by him. Dave seemed to have some degree of authority over Bobby.

MM: I was going to say at a news conference on Monday that I was pregnant. Bobby wanted an abortion, and I wanted a baby. I was going to say that I went to bed with both of them [the Kennedys] and that they used Mob people for political reasons. In AA [Alcoholics Anonymous] I was going to reform my ways. I wanted this baby. Bobby started to cry because he thought I would ruin his family name. Bobby was like a baby. I really scared him; I really got him to lose his cool. The man with Bobby said, "Let's get out of here, I will take care of this." They left. I seemed too tired to care. I thought I heard voices that I didn't recognize. They left me to die. I needed help, and they locked the door. I was having trouble remembering because I was so tired and draggy.

Q: What else do you remember about your death?

MM: I can't remember much before my death, but I can never deal with the way I died. I never meant to harm Jack because I really loved him. Jack was worried of scandal. Jackie threatened to file for a divorce. I had an affair with John after he became President. At times maybe it was a little weird. Definitely Jack took control, but Bobby liked being sweet and innocent. He wanted me to take control. Bobby liked to lay there so I would make like I would arouse him, and he would say, "Stop, stop!" Bobby liked to think he was being raped by me.

[Note: Marilyn gave us explicit details about the sexual practices between her and John. However, bowing to good taste, we have omitted this descriptive information.]

Q: We are trying to center in on your time of death. You're saying nine and ten at night, and the telephone records show that there was one call to the East Coast at about nine o'clock on the evening before you died.[3] Who was that phone call to?

MM: I didn't.

Q: You didn't call anybody?

MM: No.

Q: Did you make any phone calls after the man gave you an injection?

MM: No. I tried.

Q: Is that the time that you said you were trying to call Giancana?

MM: Yes.

Q: So the phone calls going out of your number were not made by you?

MM: No.

Q: Did they purposely make those calls to make it look like you were alive?

MM: Yes.

Q: So, in other words, after you got the injection you were not able to do too much?

MM: Yes.

Q: Peter Lawford, in the book that we are reading[4], said that it was soon after 10:00 P.M. that night that he got the final call from you. Was that true?

MM: No, not true.

Q: Dave and Bobby left together around 1:00 A.M. [August 5]. Is that true?

MM: Yeah.

Q: They left your house or they left . . .

MM: They were over at Peter's house.

Q: So, they left there together at 1:00 A.M. Are you sure that Dave went with Bobby?

MM: Yes.

Q: Did they go by helicopter?

MM: Yes.

Q: Was Dave at Peter's with Bobby all night until that helicopter flight?

MM: No. I don't know where he was.

Q: Do you know when he joined Bobby?

MM: Around midnight. I am not sure. Midnight, 1:00 A.M. Around there somewhere.

Q: Dave went somewhere else?

MM: Before that? Yeah.

Q: How long was Dave at your house? What time did he leave?

MM: Ten-thirty to eleven o'clock.

Q: I'm not sure we got that. You said he called the ambulance—the second ambulance—from somewhere else. Where was he?

MM: Peter's house.

Q: OK, they were both at Peter's, but Dave wasn't there the whole time?

MM: No.

Q: Do you know what he was doing?

MM: Um, I think he met somebody at a bar. He had a drink.

Q: With someone who had something to do with this whole thing?

MM: Yeah. I don't know who he is. He is kind of a short guy, little on the chunky side—fat side. Black, slick hair. I don't know who he is.

Q: Then Dave went back to Peter's and joined Bobby?

MM: Right.

Q: Did they talk to Peter at all?

MM: Oh, yeah.

Q: Did they tell him what went on?

MM: Oh, yeah. Ah . . . he was up all night. He was so upset!

Q: Who?

MM: Peter. Not because I died. Because he was worried about being involved.

In talking about John Kennedy:

Q: There were two men there during the later part of

the day—the older one [Tony] and the younger one with the scar on his chin [Phil]. Did John hire them?

MM: He did not make the actual call, but he spoke to Bobby, and Bobby called someone he knew to have them sent over there.

Q: Who did Bobby call?

MM: Mafia people, and Bobby promised them he wouldn't bring prosecution charges against them. But Bobby told John not to worry about it. "We don't need them, she will be dead soon."

Q: You weren't there at the time of this conversation. How do you know that this conversation took place?

MM: I just know it. Marilyn describes the men who killed her:"Black coat; black shoes; name may be Tony, but I can't seem to know more. He is an older man, about fifty. Distinguished-looking; Chicago accent; military haircut—short. Younger man about thirty-nine–forty, attractive; hair around ears; had a scar left side of chin; Chicago accent; nervous type. Both belong to Mob—freelance."

Q: We want to know about Tony. Do you want to tell us who he is? (We hold up sketch #2.) Does this sketch pretty much look like the man?

MM: Yes, definitely.

Q: Did he do anything to you, Marilyn?

MM: Yes. He created most of my bruises. I bit him. I bit him.

Q: Where did you bite him?

MM: On the hand.

Q: Why did you need to bite him?

MM: To get his hand out of my mouth.

Q: What was he doing?

MM: They squeezed my mouth open trying to shove something [pills] down my throat.

Marilyn Monroe at fifteen.
AP/WIDE WORLD PHOTOS

Marilyn Monroe at thirty-six, sex symbol and love goddess, in a shot from *Something's Got to Give,* the film she never finished.
AP/WIDE WORLD PHOTOS

"...s Cheesecake." The young actress Marilyn Monroe in 1951.
...n this photo was taken she said she would rather read
...osophy than pose for pictures like this.
...IDE WORLD PHOTOS

...ewlyweds Joe Di Maggio
...Marilyn Monroe in
...ry 1954.
...DE WORLD PHOTOS

Marilyn Monroe and Arthur
Miller at their country home in
Connecticut in 1956.
AP/WIDE WORLD PHOTOS

President John F. Kennedy and Attorney General Robert F. Kennedy, two men Marilyn knew intimately.
AP/WIDE WORLD PHOTOS

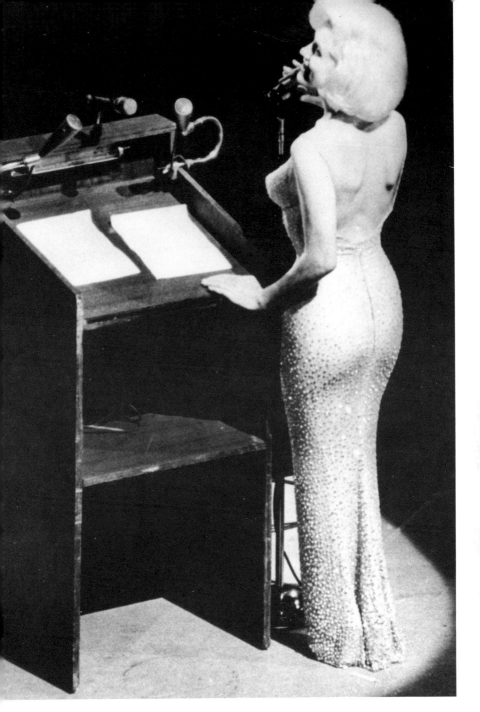

Marilyn Monroe sings "Happy Birthday" to President John F. Kennedy at Madison Square Garden on May 20, 1962.
UPI/BETTMANN

John F. Kennedy and his brother-in-law Peter Lawford in 1955.
Lawford was instrumental in Marilyn's relationships with the
Kennedy brothers.
PETER LAWFORD COLLECTION

Marilyn Monroe and Peter Lawford one week before her death.
PETER LAWFORD COLLECTION

J. Edgar Hoover meets with President Kennedy. Marilyn's spirit claims Hoover, fearful of what she might divulge at the press conference she had called for August 6, ordered her murder.

AP/WIDE WORLD PHOTOS

The spirit of Sam Giancana, infamous figure of the
Chicago underworld, claims mafia men were hired to
murder Marilyn Monroe.
AP/WIDE WORLD PHOTOS

The news reaches from coast to coast: Marilyn Monroe is dead.
UPI/BETTMANN

Marilyn's home, the set for a highly staged murder with big-name stars.
UPI/BETTMANN

The broken pane in the outside door leading into Marilyn's bedroom.

Marilyn's bedroom, where she spent the last painful, terrifying hours.
UPI/BETTMANN

Marilyn's blanket-covered body is being moved from the mortuary to the morgue.
UPI/BETTMANN

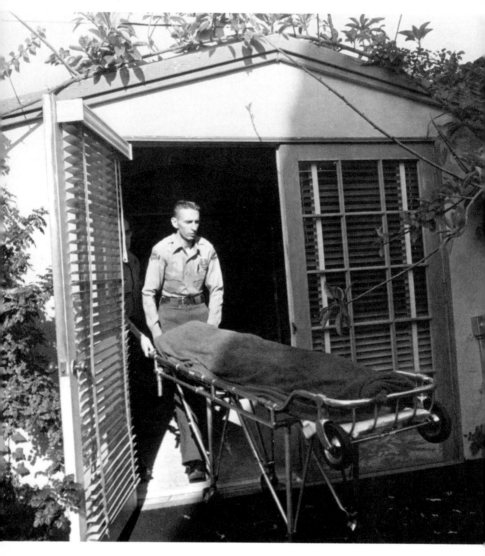

Mourners visit Marilyn's crypt.
UPI/BETTMANN

Birdie Wood's former Sanger home.
L. CANEVARI

Marilyn's crypt today. At her funeral, Lee Strasberg, her teacher and friend, said, "Marilyn Monroe was a legend. In her own lifetime she created a myth of what a poor girl from a deprived background could attain. For the entire world she became a symbol of the eternal feminine."
L. CANEVARI

Q: Did he get them down?

MM: No, they were mad because I wouldn't cram them down.

Q: What else did he do to you?

MM: Oh, he hurt me.

Q: Did he bruise you?

MM: Yes.

Q: Did he bruise you by hitting you or was it by grabbing you to maneuver you around?

MM: It was his rough hands.

Q: Where were the bruises on your body?

MM: Arms and my sides—that's all.

Q: Did you have any bruises on your legs?

MM: Could be. I don't remember.

Q: Did he put anything else in your body?

MM: Yes. He shoved something in somewhere down on my bottom. In my rear end. It just burned. I didn't feel very much after that, tired and a loss of control. I think I wet myself.

Q: Do you know what he put in your rectum?

MM: Yes, Nembutal—suppository form.

Q: Do you know what they put down your throat?

MM: No. I got very sleepy, but I could hear voices. I was being shaken around, but I couldn't speak. I felt pain. What did they do to me?

Q: Where did you feel the pain?

MM: Between my chest and stomach, a very burning sensation at first. Many black moments. Stomach eruption.

Q: Had you ever seen these men before?

MM: At a party, just acquaintance of Peter.

Q: Where was the party?

MM: In Boston hotel near the Eliot [Hotel]. He was a flunkey, and he had no importance.

Q: How long before your death was this party?

MM: Four months.

Q: Which man was there?

MM: The younger man [Phil].

97

Q: The two men who murdered you, are they still alive?

MM: Just the younger [Phil] because they had the older one [Tony] killed.

Q: Did [Phil] call the older one by name?

MM: Mac. Older one told younger one just not to be chicken-shit.

Q: Who positioned you on the bed? Did you die on your stomach or on your back?

MM: Back, because moved twice. Yes, yes, yes!

Q: From what position to what position did they move you?

MM: Put in living room.

Q: Why?

MM: Needed to clean sheets.

Q: And then they moved you a second time. Where to?

MM: Put in ambulance.

Q: What happened to you after the ambulance?

MM: Back in bed.

Q: Is this at the end?

MM: No.

Q: OK, they moved you the first time. They took you out of bed and put you in the living room to change sheets. Were you dead at the time?

MM: Yes.

Q: OK, now you're talking about an ambulance. Did ambulance people take you out of the house?

MM: Yes.

Q: Was this to go to the coroner's office?

MM: No.

Q: OK, this is something new now. Was this for Santa Monica Hospital?

MM: Yes, but they decided not—because they couldn't explain—

Q: We've visualized two ambulances, and we've never been able to explain both of them. The first one was the one you said came in about 4:30 or something, and they didn't take you out.

MM: No.

Q: When did the next car or ambulance arrive?

MM: 9:00.

Q: Was this an actual ambulance company?

MM: Yes.

Q: You were dead, and they had a second ambulance pick you up. What were they going to do with you?

MM: Take to hospital.

Q: Are you saying there were three ambulances that day?

MM: Coroner.

Q: Two ambulances and a coroner?

MM: Yes.

Q: OK, who called the ambulance?

MM: Dave.

Q: If he called, and they loaded you up to take you, then why didn't they take you?

MM: Because they couldn't explain.

Q: They couldn't explain your death. Is that what you're saying?

MM: Yes.

Q: How did the ambulance people get in your house?

MM: Window.

Q: The ambulance men came in through the window?

MM: Yes.

Q: Was there a broken window to your bedroom?

MM: Yes.

Q: Who broke it?

MM: The young man broke it.

Q: And why?

MM: Because in paying these guys off [ambulance drivers], they figured that if they were to say that they came in through an unlocked window, they

[people] would wonder why the doctor and elderly woman didn't [enter] in that window.

Q: When did the young man break it?

MM: Oh, late at night, about one o'clock in the morning.

Q: One o'clock the next morning.

MM: Yes.

Q: He fixed the window so no one knew it was broken. The first time an ambulance came, Dave
sent those two men away and they never took you
out of the bed. Is that right?

MM: Yes.

Q: Then you are saying that he decided to call them
again?

MM: Yes.

Q: Why would he have called them if he didn't know
how to explain it?

MM: Thought not dead. He got call from Bobby and
told Dave it looked too phony.

Q: Bobby told Dave it looked too phony?

MM: Yes.

Q: Bobby wasn't there, so he didn't know how it
looked. He just figured it was going to come out
phony?

MM: Yes.

Q: Did he want to stop it and try to save you?

MM: No.

Q: He just wanted to bring in some authority so it
would look like someone was trying to save you?

MM: Yes, but finally decided no good.

Q: Now you're saying you died at nine. Are you ap-
proximating?

MM: Yes. There are some things that I know, and I
don't know why I know them. There are things I
see, and I judge that I am laying down, looking
up, and I guess I was breathing. But when I am
standing up looking down, I see myself, so I've

got to be dead. Maybe I am confused, but that is the only way I can tell.

Q: So, they moved you from the ambulance back into the bed now?

MM: Yes.

Q: How were you positioned on the bed then?

MM: Stomach.

Q: Is that the position they found you in?

MM: Yes.

Q: Who put the phone in your hand?[5]

MM: I think Dave, before he finally locked the door.

Q: Were the ambulance drivers threatened to be quiet?

MM: Oh, yes.

Q: Do you know who threatened them?

MM: Dave showed his badge.

Q: What kind of badge?

MM: Government security and said it was national security.

Q: Did he actually threaten them with their lives?

MM: No, just told interfering with government.

Q: Were there any pills in the room or were all those pills brought in after you died?

MM: They were brought in later. There were no pills there.

Q: The pill bottles that they showed in the night-stand[6], were they there when you were alive?

MM: No.

Q: Where were your pills kept?

MM: They were in a box in the bathroom. I boxed them so I could clean out the bathroom. I had to have it cleaned of all my stuff.

Q: Why?

MM: They were doing something in there.

Q: Were they remodeling?

MM: Yeah.

Talking about the coroner's pick-up:

Q: Did they bring you back again, Marilyn?

MM: No.

Q: Where did they take you?

MM: Downtown.

Q: Did they take you to a hospital?

MM: No.

Q: Did they take you to the coroner's office?

MM: Lab.

Q: Who has your diary?[7]

MM: Police officer, but he disappeared.

Q: Was he CIA or FBI?

MM: Don't think so, but the man in charge of the investigation knows. He was overwhelmed by the credentials of those who took charge.

Q: Do you think you'll feel better if you release some of this frustration?

MM: Yes. I just don't want anybody to think that I tried to kill myself. I wasn't that crazy at that time.

Q: We'll make that clear. Had you tried to kill yourself before that?

MM: Yes.

Q: It's going to be hard to convince people. When was the first time you tried to kill yourself?

MM: A ways back.

Q: Do you remember?

MM: It was a ways back. Two or three years before this.

Q: What happened? What made you do that?

MM: I was panic-stricken.

Q: Did something happen that made you panic-stricken?

MM: Another person that I loved left me.

Q: Can you tell us who it was?

MM: It was Arthur [Miller], and I got the same feeling with Joe [DiMaggio]. I didn't want to live because

I couldn't let it work. There's something wrong with me.

Q: Was there something in you that wanted more?

MM: Yeah.

Q: Did you not feel worth their love?

MM: No, I really wasn't a very good person.

Q: You know, Marilyn, if you would have learned to love yourself, your relationships would have been a lot better.

MM: That's what my doctor said.

Q: Have you learned anything from this life?

MM: Don't fool around with anybody from the Kennedys!

Q: Come on, Marilyn, is that all you learned? Did you learn that it isn't right to have that many lovers?

MM: Yeah, I guess.

Q: Marilyn, were you pregnant just before you died?

MM: I was pregnant awhile before, and then I thought I was pregnant again.

Q: You had an abortion?

MM: Yes.

Q: Was that Bobby's child?

MM: Yes, the second one was.

Q: Whose was the first one?

MM: John's, but I knew I had to get rid of that because he was the President.

Q: Is that the one you aborted three months before your death?

MM: Yes.

Q: When you died you had missed your period again?

MM: Yes.

Q: You just assumed you were pregnant?

MM: Yes.

Q: But you didn't know for sure?

MM: Yes.

Q: You had a telephone conversation with Jackie, didn't you?

MM: Yes, a couple of times.

Q: She told you she would divorce John? [Refer to Chapter VII.]

MM: Yeah, more or less.

Q: But he wouldn't do that, would he?

MM: No, I'm not the only one.

Q: You're not the only one what?

MM: That had affairs with him.

Q: Bobby didn't fool around as much as John, though.

MM: Yeah.

Q: Do you know why they would risk their high places to have affairs? Why would they risk looking so bad to the public?

MM: Because it was important to them to have affairs. It made them feel important.

Q: So they liked the riskiness and danger of it?

MM: Yeah, they also like women.

Q: Like father, like son?

MM: Yeah, the old man wanted to go to bed with me, but he was too old.

Q: That's all the questions we have at this time. Do you have anything else you need to share with us tonight? Are you going to be able to see us another time if we need you?

MM: I don't think I can . . . I have to be going . . . I did what I asked to do. I appreciate you spending the time. It's only the fans that really like me. Nobody else liked me.

Q: Are you going to be moving on soon?

MM: I hope so.

Q: We were hoping that we would get to see you, that you could show yourself. You were going to look into that.

MM: I forgot.

Q: We are going to try to contact you once more, so between now and then, can you check it out?

MM: Yes. Do you know if they are going to call for another opening on this case?

Q: Not at this point. We don't know anything about that. They may after our book is out. Who knows? Would you like that?

MM: Yes.

Q: Is there something that you wanted to say before we let you go?

MM: I wish I could get through to Bob.

Q: Bobby [Kennedy]?

MM: No.

Q: Bob Slatzer?

MM: Yes. I feel sorry for him.

Q: Do you know how we can contact him? [Note: Mr. Slatzer is still alive.]

MM: Yes.

Q: He is open to that, isn't he?

MM: He's too fidgety . . . too nervous . . . too emotional.

Q: We would very much like to talk to him, if you could whisper in his ear. Were you married to him?

MM: Yeah.

Q: Marilyn, we think he still cares about you and would be very interested in helping us with this if we could get through to him . . . if you can help us with that. We don't know where to start.

MM: You know this guy that he hired is running into a dead end. Ask him to forward a letter.

Q: What guy is that?

MM: The one that was running all over trying to find out what happened. He's got my picture above his head . . . Yeah, he likes me. I think he likes me. He's kind of infatuated with me.

Q: What's his name?

MM: His first name is Milo.

Q: Do you know his last name?

MM: Oh, Spiglio or something.

Q: Is it Speriglio?

MM: Could be. He don't have the whole story. I want him to put it right.

Q: Do you know who he thinks killed you?

MM: Yeah, he thinks it was Sam [Giancana] and Johnny, and it wasn't.

Q: Johnny who?

MM: Roselli.

Q: Do you think Milo would forward a letter to Bob [Slatzer]?

MM: Could be.

Q: What is Speriglio's profession?

MM: He's a detective.

Q: Is there some code word that we could tell Bob so that he would know that we are for real?

MM: Tell him, "Remember our car ride." Tell Bob he needs to calm down. He will have problems if he doesn't, health problems.

Q: We plan to write Bob c/o Milo, we would like to give him some kind of hint.

MM: I talked to him a lot before all this happened. I mean I told him a lot. I needed someone that I could trust, and I knew I could trust him. He's very open to spirits and stuff. He'll cooperate.

Q: Where was your car ride to?

MM: Why do you want to know?

Q: If it's really personal, you don't have to tell us. We just thought if we could tell him, "Remember the car ride to . . . somewhere," it might jog his memory.

MM: You can tell him, "Remember the car ride by the water."

Q: We had an idea from talking to some of our spirit friends . . .

MM: Yes, yes . . .

Q: That you may have had a part in calling some people to the "other side" before their time. Are you working on anyone else at this point? Are you through with that? Is that true to begin with?

MM: Yeah. I feel better now.

Q: Did you do that out of anger?

MM: Yeah.

Q: Is that all that's going to happen?

MM: I don't know . . . see how I feel.

Q: Hope we are on your good list.

MM: Yeah.

Thank you for helping us. Goodbye, Marilyn.

CHAPTER VI

CONVERSATIONS WITH PETER LAWFORD

PETER LAWFORD
September 7, 1923 to December 24, 1984

Peter Lawford and Marilyn Monroe met somewhere around 1950. Peter was an established movie star, and Marilyn was still struggling. They were never romantically involved, but they remained friends throughout her life. It was through Peter that Marilyn was introduced to Jack and Bobby Kennedy.[1,2]

SESSION: July 27, 1990

On the night of July 27, 1990, we were gathered for our regular weekly meeting. Before beginning we were casually discussing, in a joking manner, who we would like to make contact with in the spirit world if we were allowed the opportunity to select. Everyone agreed that Peter Lawford would be an important figure due to his close involvement with Marilyn Monroe and his alleged inside knowledge of the people involved in her death. There was also the theory that he himself played a pivotal role in the cover-up.

We then organized ourselves into a formal circle and began to clear our thoughts and concentrate on the Ouija board before us. Much to our surprise, a spirit identifying itself as Peter Lawford came on the board immediately. We followed our established procedure of asking that he provide identifying information. He gave us his birth date of September 7, 1923, which we later verified.[3] We explained to Peter that at Marilyn Monroe's request we were trying to compile an accurate account of the events surrounding her death and hoped he would help us. Peter replied that he didn't want to tell on his friends, and therefore we would not get much information from him. He added that he

110

only came on the board out of curiosity and didn't have much to say.

After considerable coaxing, Peter agreed to help us based on his friendship with Marilyn. He admitted that he had contact with both John and Bobby Kennedy on the date of Marilyn's death (August 4, 1962) and had himself gone to her house the morning of August 5.

We asked Peter to take us back to August 4, 1962, at his house and tell us what happened that day. We asked for as many details as possible, e.g., who he had talked to, who came to his house, and what he himself did. He provided us with the following sequence of events.

At approximately 8:30 A.M. Peter received a phone call from John Kennedy to tell him that he was needed. More precisely, his house was needed—to be "a center"—for the activities that were to follow that day because "Marilyn Monroe was to go."

Next, Peter received a call from Bobby Kennedy around 9:00 A.M. Bobby was calling from San Francisco to say he had to see Marilyn and needed Peter's help. Peter made the necessary arrangements and provided Bobby with a place to stay that night at his beach house, which was relatively near Marilyn's home.

President Kennedy called again about 12:30 P.M. hoping Bobby would be there, but he had not yet arrived. The third call from John Kennedy came around 1:30 P.M. He didn't converse with Peter but talked directly with Bobby, who had arrived by then. Peter didn't know the details of this conversation, only that Jack and Bobby discussed the "trip to Marilyn's."

Bobby flew in on August 4, landing in a helicopter at

Peter's home. This evoked a series of questions and answers with Peter:

Q: What time did he land?
PL: 1:00 P.M.
Q: Was anyone with him when he arrived?
PL: No, he was alone.
Q: What time did he go to Marilyn's house?
PL: Around 2:00 P.M.
Q: How did he get from your house to Marilyn's house?
PL: By car and driver—a man who had driven Bobby and Marilyn around a number of times before. [Note: Bobby made a stop along the way to Marilyn's to pick up a man called "Dave."]
Q: What time did he leave to go back to San Francisco?
PL: I really don't want to say.
Q: We need this information—you are very important in all of this.
PL: Don't remind me!
Q: Do you still feel badly about it all?
PL: Yes.
Q: Did Bobby come back to your house?
PL: Yes.
Q: What time did he get back to your house?
PL: Around 3:30 or 4:00 P.M.

Peter went on to say that Bobby remained at his home the rest of that day. He kept to himself, stationing himself in a section of the house where he answered numerous phone calls. There was a prearranged code for incoming calls to cue Peter when to answer; all other calls Bobby took himself. Peter emphasized that "you have to understand that priorities came first every time," and this applied anytime Bobby was there.

Bobby did have some visitors. A car arrived with some men in the afternoon. Peter says he has no idea who these men were, partly because he had been drinking. To further complicate matters for Peter, he and his wife had invited a few friends over that evening. Peter stated "there was too much to deal with," but he felt it would have been "too phony" to cancel the party.

At some point during the night Dave arrived. Peter was quite guarded initially and hesitant to give us much information on Dave. He first said he was never introduced to him but had accidentally heard Bobby mention his first name. Peter was under the impression that Dave worked for the government because he had some authority over Bobby. Peter was unsure but thought he was either from the FBI or CIA. Dave was "kind of scolding [Bobby] for telling Marilyn that John wanted to use the bomb on South America." He was referring to the atomic bomb and talking of using it on Castro's Cuba and other Communist strongholds. This is an example of the highly confidential information Marilyn had that finally got her into serious trouble.

Peter withheld any further information on Dave, feeling it would be better if we didn't know, but he did finally tell us that this man worked for the "FBI and used [the name] Dave when working on Hoover assignments." He added that there are things that he knows that we cannot know for our own good.

Bobby and Dave finally left Peter's house after midnight on the dawning of August 5. They left in the helicopter, heading for the Los Angeles airport, and from there Bobby would fly back to San Francisco. Peter states that he first learned that Marilyn was dead when he overheard Dave talking to Bobby before they left his house. He believes that was around 11:30 P.M.

According to Summers in *Goddess* (p. 401), "Reporter Joe Hyams tried to track down the helicopter said to have landed at the beach on the night of the tragedy. At an aircraft rental company, he established that 'a small helicopter had been rented on the night of Marilyn's death. But the company was not willing to allow me access to the records and flatly refused to tell me the name of the passenger. I was, in fact, warned off the premises.'" However, photographer William Woodfield found an entry in the company's log showing a helicopter had been rented to pick up a passenger at the Lawford house taking him to the main Los Angeles airport. The time, he believed, was between midnight and 2:00 A.M. The log clearly showed that a helicopter had picked up Robert Kennedy at the Santa Monica beach.[4]

We asked Peter to tell us about his own contacts with Marilyn on August 4, wondering if he was possibly the last person to talk to her (by phone) before she died. He confirmed that Marilyn kept calling his home, but the last time was around 6:00 P.M., and he didn't speak with her himself because he knew what was happening. Peter went on to say that he was asked to go to Marilyn's house after her death to go through her files and papers. The request came from John Kennedy on behalf of the Kennedys and the government. President Kennedy had called Peter from Washington that morning and from Hyannis Port in the afternoon.

Peter did go over to Marilyn's house on August 5 at approximately 5:00 A.M. When he arrived, the doctor

114

was still there along with a few policemen. Marilyn's body had already been removed. Outside there were some "studio people" and some reporters. Peter was allowed inside after telling them he was there to make funeral arrangements and to make some calls. But instead, he opened Marilyn's files and went through her papers. He pulled out some "love mail and cards" which he later burned. Then by accident he left Marilyn's controversial diary on top of a pile of papers and unknowingly gave it to the district attorney's office. According to Peter, the D.A.'s office subsequently removed the diary from their official records under orders from government men working for J. Edgar Hoover.

We tried to delve a little more deeply into the feelings Peter had about what happened that night. He responded by saying that he had felt extremely guilty during the remainder of his life but was afraid to speak out. Peter was afraid of being branded as a murderer. He also confirmed that Bobby had an affair with Marilyn Monroe but didn't love her. Quite the contrary, Bobby thought Marilyn was a "slut, but he liked fucking her." However, Peter believes that John really cared for Marilyn. He added that they all (including himself) liked the excitement of "living on the edge." Then, after it was all over, everyone lied to cover up their own involvement.

We next displayed our sketch of the man who arrived at Marilyn's house with Tony. We hoped Peter would be able to identify him for us. Peter admitted he had attended a party at a Boston hotel at which this man and Marilyn were present. He told us he didn't know the name of the hotel because he was "high," and pointed out that it does not affect our material. He advised that the man's name is "Phil." Peter described Phil as having long hair—"like a girl"—and because of this "he had a nickname about fruit." He is Italian and belonged to the Mafia in Chicago. He was assigned to "go with Tony" because he is the nephew of some "big shot in the Mob."

We asked if there is anyone living whom we could contact to help us in our search for the truth. Peter replied that no one will get involved except Marilyn's alleged ex-husband, Bob Slatzer.

Out of curiosity, we asked Peter how he could possibly know these things. He replied, "We talk here, too, and I have my head cleared here, even though I can't feel it."

Another point we wanted clarified during this session concerned a letter that Marilyn allegedly wrote to him the day she died. Peter confirmed the existence of such a letter in which Marilyn wanted to threaten him so he would encourage Bobby to continue his relationship with her. The threat she used was that she would "tell all" about Peter's drug addiction.

The Ouija board was slowing down to a very sluggish movement, and it seemed that Peter was tiring. We asked if he had seen Marilyn in the spirit world. He replied sadly that he had not because he doesn't want to face her, and "they" respect his wishes.

At this point Peter advised us that he had to go— that he had already talked too much. He indicated he would be willing to come back another time to answer a few more questions.

SESSION: August 20, 1990

On this evening we had communicated briefly with an entity identifying itself as Sidney Skolsky (see Chapter VII). Unexpectedly, Peter came on the board explaining that he wanted to clarify some statements that a spirit identifying itself as Fred Karger made to us (on August 14, 1990). Karger had informed us that by using whatever influence she had been given in the spirit world, Marilyn had fashioned a "hit list" of sorts, as a means of getting even with those people directly and indirectly responsible for her death (see Chapter VII).

Peter revealed to us that he did see Marilyn just before he died. She was present in his hospital room, and he had the definite feeling that she came to get him. He went on to say that he died a very painful death, just like "his buddies" (the Kennedys) did. The difference was that his was a slow process. His wife at the time was Pat Seaton Lawford, and she was with him when he died. In her book, Seaton states that Peter had been in a coma and was on life-support equipment. Then, suddenly, on December 24, 1984, "at 8:50 A.M., there was movement. Peter's body rose, as though he were struggling into a push-up position, and suddenly blood rushed from every opening. His heart stopped.

117

His lungs stopped" . . . "Peter Lawford was dead."
(Lawford, 1988, p. 239–240)[5] Could it be that Peter
was aware of Marilyn's presence, that she had come to
get him, and he was rising up to meet her?

Pat Seaton's book is allegedly based on the manuscript Peter had been working on prior to his death.
Peter acknowledged to us that he died broke, leaving
his wife nothing. Therefore, as a means of generating
money, she wrote *The Peter Lawford Story*. Peter indicated he wasn't too pleased with the book, and that she
had no real facts or direct personal knowledge of how
Marilyn Monroe died. He disclosed that there were fi-
nancial dealings made to portray Jack and Bobby Kennedy in a more favorable light and to indicate that they
had nothing to do with Marilyn's death. Apparently,
according to Peter, the Kennedy family had earlier tried
to influence him as to how he proposed to handle the
relationship between Marilyn and the Kennedys in his
manuscript. He had not been willing to bow to their
wishes because "the boys" were already gone, and, with
them, a certain amount of his allegiance.

We wondered if Peter or any of our other spirit ac-
quaintances were currently helping anyone else to write
a book on Marilyn. He assured us they are not.

According to Peter, there were two other celebrities
who knew the circumstances of Marilyn's death. They
had learned this information from their association
with Sam Giancana. The specific details are being
withheld as these two famous people are still alive.

On a more solemn note, Peter said that he loved
Marilyn, too, in his own way. He is presently on "level
one," the lowest level in the spirit world. The reason
for this is based on the lifestyle he led during his life on

earth. In his own words, "I did it all!" He further advised that he is limited in how many times he can communicate with us, so, sadly, our time with him will be running out soon. He wanted us to know that Birdie's role (Birdie Wood) was like that of an ambassador, but there was a higher spirit force that decided how these revelations would be handled. He explained that there are reasons for information to come out at certain times. All things are planned ahead; we were at the right time and the right place.

SESSION: September 10, 1990

As usual, we were all gathered at 6:30 P.M., and, while we ate a light dinner, we discussed the progress we were making and how we should begin to pull our collected information together into a readable storyline. We also laughed about a front-page article which had appeared this week in one of the scandal tabloids announcing that Marilyn Monroe had been found alive and was living in Newdegate, Australia.[6] Accompanying the *Sun* article, published on September 11, 1990, was a photograph of a wrinkled, aging woman who did bear some resemblance to what Marilyn Monroe might have looked like had she maintained her self-abusive life style and reached the age of sixty-four. We felt that the article was, at least, as bizarre as are the tabloid stories claiming that Elvis Presley is alive and hiding out.

We approached tonight's session with some trepidation, remembering our unusual and alarming episode last week. On September 3, 1990, Marilyn's spirit had entered Lee's (Leonore Canevari, one of the authors) body suddenly, and without warning or permission, had caused Lee to collapse into deep sobs and endure some physical discomfort. As experienced as Lee is, she had never encountered anything like this before and didn't want to repeat the ordeal.

We all agreed that we didn't want to work with the Ouija board any more often than necessary and would therefore limit its use at future meetings. Despite warnings from other psychics, we were curious enough to want to try to make contact with one more powerful figure from Marilyn's past: Sam Giancana. So, we took extra precautions this night by calling for the protective white light to surround us and protect us, and specifically asked that no spirit be allowed to enter our bodies without prior permission.

Then, as suddenly as he had once before, Peter Lawford came on the board. He seemed in very "good spirits" and obliged us by repeating his birth date and giving us his date of death. He humorously chided us, pretending to be disappointed because we had failed to wish him a happy birthday three days earlier on September 7. He added that they don't celebrate birthdays where he is. We told Peter that we would like to contact Giancana, however, he quickly vetoed the plan, stating that he didn't see "the bum," but would try to get him for us next week.

We asked why he had come to us again tonight. Peter replied that he is lonely, and had overheard our dinner conversation and apparently felt free to join us in discussion of the tabloid article. When asked how he knew about the *Sun* story, he answered that he read our thoughts. He also explained that he had originally heard this plan developed at his home by the Kennedys a few months after Marilyn's death. We asked if there was any truth to the story, and he answered "yes and no." He assured us that Marilyn is deceased. However, the plot reported in the article had actually been an "alternative plan" for dealing with Marilyn's death which was conceived by the Kennedys and government agents. This current news release had apparently been "leaked" to the public now because people are getting too close to the truth about Marilyn's murder, and those responsible are afraid the real facts may come out.

The *Sun* article reports that the Kennedy administration had Marilyn Monroe doped up and secretly transported to Australia. They kept her heavily medicated and hidden to stop her from disclosing to the American public her affairs with the Kennedys. Other secret information she allegedly had on the Kennedys would have ended their political careers and could damage the Democratic party.

Apparently, according to Peter, there *is* a Monroe lookalike in Australia—a woman who underwent reconstructive surgery to create a resemblance to Marilyn. Her fingerprints were even destroyed by burning. She is drug-addicted and brainwashed. The incredible thing about this scheme was that it was *not* an alternative plan to killing Marilyn. It was conceived in case it was someday proven that Marilyn was murdered. In that event they could reveal this woman in Australia and try to pass her off as Marilyn Monroe. The government was betting on the fact that the public would never buy the idea that Marilyn was murdered and on the premise that the police department and the grand jury in Los Angeles would never consider reopening the case.

This plan was allegedly conceived by the Kennedys because Bobby had panicked due to his concerns that the public would become aware of his involvement with Marilyn and her death. The Kennedys felt that people would not chastise them for hiding Marilyn out, and John Kennedy would say it was for the good of the country.

[Note: During this discussion we began to have a problem with the planchette (the speller piece of the Ouija board), feeling an unusually heavy push causing it to make a scratching noise due to the force moving it. We called this to Peter's attention, and the pressure was immediately lightened.]

We all concluded that this article about the Marilyn imposter was something we did not have to concern ourselves with, so we moved on to other issues. We wondered if Peter knew why Marilyn had been so upset at our last contact, at which time she sobbed uncontrollably. Peter replied that Marilyn still has problems because "she refuses to let go." We commented that it seems to us that every spirit we have contacted has been as emotionally involved as Marilyn. Peter quipped that this isn't so, pointing out that "the doctor" is not keen to have it all out, the Kennedys ain't too thrilled, you know that I don't want my reputation darkened, and Gladys [Marilyn's mother who was mentally unstable] doesn't know what she wants."

We asked Peter about some photos that he allegedly took of Marilyn and Jack Kennedy while involved in sexual acts.[7] We were curious as to their whereabouts. Peter indicated that someone may be using them to blackmail the Kennedys.

We again questioned Peter about what spiritual level or plane he is on. Here again his sense of humor emerged as he replied that he is on a very low level, so low, in fact, "I don't think they even know I am here." Peter added, "I love you girls." He continues to think of himself as a "ladies' man". Since we were in a happy mood, we asked if he has any contact with the dog, Asta, who appeared with him in *The Thin Man* television series. He hasn't seen Asta, but added "We have a dogy [doggie] heaven," and, in fact, a heaven for all animals.

We told Peter that we had watched one of his early movies on TV recently—*Good News*—and commented how young and handsome he was in the movie. Peter agreed and, referring to his fans, added that "all the other women think the same thing."

Finally, we inquired about Birdie Wood, with whom we hadn't had contact for some time. Peter stated clearly that Birdie does not need to talk to our group; she's not needed anymore for contact; she is "off the case."

SESSION: October 15, 1990

By this time we had received and compiled a great deal of information but still found ourselves unclear about one of the people (the women, Adele) who participated in Marilyn's murder on August 4, 1962. We decided to call upon our spirit entities to ask for guidance in revisualizing this especially painful scene.

Once again, it was Peter who responded. He said he came to help us with the visualization because he still feels very guilty. He reasoned that "I am not a murderer by nature, I only took part."

We wondered how he could help us revisualize this particularly ghastly scene when he had not been there himself. Peter explained that he heard the whole story from Dave on August 4, 1962. Peter did help with the revisualization, and that information has been incorporated into Chapter IV. He then made a request of us to "be nice to me in the book."

After Peter had bid us goodbye, much to our surprise Birdie Wood came on the board. We asked if she had something to tell us. She replied, "Please make sure you include me in your farewell." She added that this will be important to every one of our spirit friends, and they will all be able to come—if it is a farewell.

We asked if it would be possible for any of our spirit contacts to materialize. We were particularly hoping to see Marilyn and Peter. Her response was that she didn't know if it would be allowed because they all talked too much.

SESSION: December 1, 1990

This session was a special one because it was to be our last contact with Peter. We had prepared a list of specific questions concerning the events that took place at his home on August 4, 1962. We needed to clarify as precisely as possible the sequence of contacts he had with President Kennedy and Bobby Kennedy, as well as with Dave and Marilyn herself. Peter was very cooperative as usual and provided most of the information we needed. This data has been incorporated into the session of July 27, 1990, for continuity of reading.

It was at this time that Peter let us know that "we can't go on much longer," and in fact he thought he might have to leave during this contact. He explained simply that "our time is short." He felt that "MM must go on. It is her time to sit in silence."

We asked Peter if he has had any contact with Jack

and Bobby Kennedy in the spirit realm. He said he never sees them because they are in a "different place." Even if he could, he would choose not to see them. We asked if he thought President Kennedy would talk to us about his assassination at some later time. He answered "yes."

We told Peter we are planning a little farewell party as soon as our writing is finished. We hoped they would all be able to be with us so we can express our wonderment and appreciation for having been chosen for this project.

CHAPTER VII

RELEVANT SPIRIT CONTACTS

FRED KARGER
1916 to 1979

Fred Karger met Marilyn Monroe in 1948. He was
said to be thirty-two years old and Marilyn twenty-one.
He was her vocal coach at Columbia Pictures. In addition to teaching her how to sing, Karger arranged for
Marilyn to move into the Hollywood Studio Club, and
he helped finance the cosmetic dental work done on
her front teeth. He introduced her to fine literature
and classical music but did not return the love she had
for him. Karger died of leukemia on August 5, 1979,
exactly seventeen years after Marilyn's death.[1]

After a lengthy conversation with the spirit of Marilyn Monroe on August 14, 1990, she agreed to put Fred Karger on the Board. At our request Fred told us he was older than Marilyn and was born in 1921. (Research suggests he was born circa 1916.) He gave his date of death as August 5, 1979 (verified). However, when we asked for his wife's name, he replied, "I cannot remember very much. I know I had a kid, and I can't remember what he looked like. I [know] I am almost out of my body again. I cannot become spirit. I must forget again. I was told it is time to forget."

When we asked about levels, he replied that Marilyn is on level 2 (from the bottom), and he is on level 5, explaining that while on the Earth plane he was a pretty good guy. He believes there are about twenty levels in all.

Since passing over, he has not seen Marilyn but believes she has seen his mother, Annie. He somehow has been given the understanding that he will meet Marilyn again and discover her again in their next reincarnation. Their common bond will be music. He feels he will be coming back soon and will be another "music man, because I recently met a musician, and he thought I was very good." Marilyn will also come back one of these days as a struggling artist. Karger mused, "Can we deal with another Marilyn Monroe?"

On a more eerie note, Karger revealed that it was no coincidence that he died in the same month and on the same day as Marilyn. She arranged it "because she always wanted me." We asked if there was anything else we should know. He advised that she also called the doctor. She has the ability to play with a person's mind. "She appears to them, and they panic if they did bad things." He suggested that we look at the pattern of all the people who were connected to her. For instance, "Peter [Lawford] died saying her name. His death was awful, especially the days before—he suffered." Also Milton Greene. [Milton Greene died of cancer on August 5, 1985.[2]] In fact, Karger offered a warning: "Tell her supposed friends 'beware' ", and he specifically named two individuals whose identities we cannot reveal.

We wondered if he foresaw any trouble ahead for us as a result of writing this book. He replied, "Not if you do it for good. You seem to be people that want to bring out wrongdoing. Be patient, you will make people think. Marilyn Monroe agreed to talk to you when many have tried. Keep doing your plans. Goodbye."

SIDNEY SKOLSKY
May 2, 1905 to May 3, 1983

Sidney Skolsky was a Hollywood columnist and reporter for over fifty years. He befriended Marilyn Monroe in the late 1940's and became one of her strongest promoters and her lifelong confidant. He kept Marilyn's name in the columns and escorted her around town to keep her on public display. In 1954, he wrote a biography about his friend entitled *Marilyn.* Marilyn continued to rely on and confide in Skolsky until her death.[3]

Again on the Ouija board, we asked if anyone wanted to speak with us. Sidney Skolsky came on the board. He provided his birth date as May 2, 1905 (verified), and his date of death as May 3, 1983 (verified). He boldly stated, "Tonight is my night." His contact with us was brief and to the point:

SS: Find time to get those bastards . . . the Kennedys. I used to like them. Marilyn knew what would happen. I told her to be careful.

Q: When was the last time you spoke to her?

SS: Friday [August 3, 1962]. I think that was the day. She told me she was being followed, and she was getting funny phone calls. People would call all night long, so she would get no sleep and take more pills. She thought they were just trying to scare her to break off relations because of Hoover. I know what a cover-up it was.

Sidney Skolsky left the board as quickly as he had appeared.

GLADYS BAKER
May 24, 1900 to March 11, 1984

Gladys Pearl Monroe, Marilyn Monroe's mother, was born in Diaz, Mexico, on May 24, 1900. She had two children, Hermitt Jack and Bernice, by her first husband, Jack Baker. Gladys's family had a history of emotional problems. She herself was diagnosed as a paranoid schizophrenic and spent many years in hospitals and sanitariums. She and Marilyn lived together very little. At the age of seventy, she was able to move to a retirement home. She died in Gainesville, Florida, on March 11, 1984.[4]

Our first contact with Gladys was quite unexpected, though in the course of our investigation for this book, the unexpected should be the expected! It was clear there was an entity on the Ouija board that evening of August 20, 1990, but the initial communication made no sense. For example, the following was spelled out on the Board: YES DK KG S NO M PI YES ISKTJ YES NO W NO FRIEND OF MM GOOD NO DIWJ NO YES.

Q: Date of death?
A: 3/24/84. [Verified as 3/11/84.]

Q: Born?

A: 5/24/1900 [verified]. Gladys Pearl Marilyn Baker Mortenson. I loved MM. She didn't forgive me, and she sent me back.

Q: Back to the hospital?

GB: Yes.

Q: What didn't she forgive you for?

GB: Leaving her.

Q: Do you have a message for us?

GB: Yes. Watched me die.

Q: Marilyn?

GB: Yes, I saw her.

Q: Was Marilyn at your deathbed?

GB: Yes.

Q: Did she cause your death?

GB: No.

Q: She was just there to welcome you?

GB: Take me home.

Q: So, she only had good intentions when she came to get you?

GB: Yes.

Q: Do you believe that she could have anything to do with other people's death—in a bad way?

GB: She can be like that.

Q: Why are people saying Marilyn Monroe is appearing to them at their time of death?

GB: Their deaths. Yes, yes! [Your] book to tell them.

Q: How does she have so much control?

GB: Sex appeal. Yes. Men in charge. A mother's way of saying a story. No harm to others. Just to remind them that it's time to repay what they did to her—planned to get rid of her.

Q: Why did you contact us?

GB: To apologize for MM leaving.

Q: Where did you die?

GB: Florida [verified].

Q: Where were you born?

GB: Diaz, Mexico [verified].

Q: What are your other kids' names?

GB: Daughter, Bernice; son, Jack. Husband—Hermitt Baker, middle name Jack. Don't you believe in anything? Also crazy, and I don't have anything to say except, "Get Bobby—the prick."

Q: Do you know who Marilyn's father is?

GB: No . . . Gil Gunter . . . attractive man . . . worked with me in film industry. Kept a picture of him. MM had it.

Q: Can you come back to us again?

GB: Yes.

Q: Why did you have such problems getting on the board?

GB: Died all mixed up as to who I was. Goodbye.

ROBERT FRANCIS KENNEDY
November 20, 1925 to June 5, 1968

    Robert Kennedy was a United States senator and the Attorney General in the administration of his brother, John F. Kennedy. He was assassinated during his 1968 race for the Democratic presidential nomination.[5] It is believed Robert began an affair with Marilyn Monroe in 1962—in the months preceding her death.[6]

    The session on August 27, 1990, also began with gibberish on the board, but then settled down.

Q: Anyone on board?
A: Mama.
Q: Name?
A: Gladys.
Q: Can you get someone for us?
GB: Who?
Q: One of the Kennedys?
GB: Why? [pause] OK.

The initials "BK" were spelled out.
Q: Bobby?
A: Yes.
Q: Birth date?
BK: I don't want to give you anything. I didn't choose to be here.
Q: You don't want to answer?
BK: Not till I talk to my brother—not going to make your book more sellable.
Q: Do you know who killed Jack [John F. Kennedy]?
BK: Not answering.
Q: Why did you come on the board?
BK: Asked.
Q: Can't you say no?
BK: I want you to know that we will not be exploited.
Q: Can we make a deal?
BK: Yes.
Q: Will you come on the board next week after you talk to Jack?
BK: Yes.
Q: Why do you have to talk to him?
BK: That's what I want to do. Not until I talk to Jack. Why do you keep asking questions? Tonight go to bed. I will. Goodbye.

As suddenly as Bobby left, Gladys returned to the board saying, "They think I am crazy even here!"

JOHN FITZGERALD KENNEDY
May 29, 1917 to November 22, 1963

As a World War II hero, John Kennedy was awarded the Purple Heart in 1943. He was elected to Congress in 1946 and won election to the U.S. Senate in 1952. He went on to become the thirty-fifth president of the United States.[7] He became acquainted with Marilyn Monroe in the early 1950's, and their relationship continued until shortly before her death in August 1962. He was killed by an assassin's bullet fifteen months after her death.[8]

Continuing our pattern, we gathered again the following week to follow up our contact with Robert Kennedy. After our usual meditation and preparation, the letters BK were spelled out on the Ouija board.

Q: Bobby Kennedy?
A: Yes.
Q: Are you going to talk with us tonight?
BK: No.
Q: Did you check with John [Kennedy]?
BK: Yes.
Q: What did he say?
BK: He will talk.

Q: OK, let us know when John comes on the board. Go to your initials. [We concentrate on John's face, and the planchette moves to "Yes" on the board.] Can we have your initials?

A: JK.

Q: What was your date of birth?

JK: 5/29/1917 [verified].

Q: How about the date of your death?

JK: 11/22/1963 [verified].

Q: John, do you know why we contacted you?

JK: Yes. I am not going to answer anything unless I want to.

Q: Are you willing to help us in any way?

JK: It depends.

Q: It depends on what?

JK: On questions.

Q: Is there anything you would like to clear up?

JK: No.

Q: John, we're here mainly to talk to you about Marilyn's death and the circumstances surrounding how she died. Can you fill in any blanks on that issue?

JK: I don't think so.

Q: Why did you come on the board?

JK: So Bobby doesn't have to.

Q: Do you know who was behind your death?

JK: Government.

Q: Was it basically the C.I.A.?

JK: More.

Q: Did the Secret Service have anything to do with it?

JK: Not really.

Q: Do you know who actually ordered your death?

JK: No.

Q: Is there anything you would like to share with us about your death? Did Lee Harvey Oswald kill you? Did he shoot you?

JK: No.

Q: Were the shots fired from the grassy knoll from behind the fence?

JK: Yes. Group

Q: It was a conspiracy—a group of people?

JK: Yes.

Q: Mostly in our own government?

JK: Yes.

Q: Was Castro, the plot to kill him, and the Mafia involved with your death?

JK: Yes.

[Note: The Mafia was strong in Louisiana and virtually controlled the state. Its leaders have been linked to Kennedy's assassination.[9]

Q: OK. Can we ask you some questions about Marilyn Monroe?

JK: Maybe.

The answer "Maybe" seemed better than a flat "No." So we started to probe into the area of his connection with Marilyn Monroe.

The entity identifying itself as President John F. Kennedy went on to admit that he had an affair with Marilyn that began before he became President. He recalled that he met Marilyn soon after he married Jackie. He believes he first met Marilyn in 1954. Bobby became involved with Marilyn after John decided not to see her again. We took it one step further hoping he would be honest with us when we asked, "Did you really love Marilyn?" His reply was "yes."

President Kennedy referred to Jackie as a "payment

wife," in that the marriage was for appearance and for having children. Jackie knew about his affair with Marilyn, and in fact had received phone calls in which Marilyn suggested she (Jackie) consider divorcing John.

Q: Give us the date of your wedding.
JK: 9/20/53 [Verified as 9/12/53[10]].
Q: When was Carolyn born? [Daughter]
JK: 11/20/1957 [Verified as 11/27/57[11]].
Q: When was John Jr. born? [Son]
JK: 11/19/60 [Verified as 11/25/60[12]].
Q: Is this the first time you've contacted anyone on the Ouija board?
JK: Yes.
Q: Have other people tried?
JK: No.
Q: Were you aware of the planning that was going into Marilyn's death?
JK: Don't need to answer.
Q: Was there anything you could have done to stop it?
JK: No.
Q: Was she murdered basically because of your family name? Or was it more in the line of—for the good of the country?
JK: I didn't say she was murdered.
Q: Marilyn told us she was. Are you saying that she wasn't murdered?
JK: No comment.
Q: Was she planning to do something to ruin your family, your reputation, and the reputation of the Democratic party?
JK: Could be.
Q: Something you don't want to talk about?
JK: No.
Q: Did you discuss with her what happened at the Bay of Pigs?

JK: Don't need to answer.
Q: Do you feel guilty about anything that went on?
JK: No.
Q: Murder is murder—for whatever reason. How do you handle it in that context?
JK: I will pay.
Q: If you have to pay, do you have to make it up to her in another lifetime?
JK: I don't know.
Q: What level are you on up there?
JK: Higher than her!
Q: Do you know how many levels there are? Give us a number?

We had to break here as there was a problem with Lee. She began sobbing and moaning, rocking in her chair. The crying continued as we asked her the following questions:

Q: What's happening? Share what's happening.
L: Why are you talking to him? (It was apparently Marilyn talking through Lee.)
Q: You don't want us to talk to him? You'll have to share it with us, Marilyn. Calm down. Talking to him is hurting you?
MM: He don't care!
Q: OK, we'll let him go. We won't talk to him if it's bothering you.
MM: I can see him!
Q: Is it better to let him go? Do you want to dismiss him? We think he's gone. Do you see him anymore?
MM: No. I have pain in my stomach. (Lee is crying and doubled over at this point.)
Q: What's the pain from? Tell us.
MM: I don't know.
Q: Are you going back to your death scene, Marilyn?

Marilyn, you need to leave now—you're going to make Lee sick. Can you calm down? Take deep breaths. John's gone, and we'll have you go back for tonight. Are you still here, Marilyn?

MM: Yes.

Q: Can you try to say something without getting upset? This is very strenuous for Lee.

MM: Yes.

Q: Go ahead—we're listening. Are you calm now?

MM: Yes.

Q: We're here for you. Calm down. Tell us what you have to.

MM: Everyone thinks I'm no good!

Q: Who thinks that? We don't think that. There are a lot of people out there that have followed you for a long time. They care about what happened. They still love you after thirty years.

MM: I couldn't help myself.

Q: How is it you came to us tonight? Did you know John was here? Is that why you came?

MM: Yes. My mother told me.

Q: Your mom came to tell you?

MM: I hate him!

Q: You hate who? John?

MM: Yes. [Marilyn (Lee) becomes upset again.]

Q: What do you need to tell us? Get calm again. Did you want us to get rid of him?

MM: Don't believe him! He knows! He knows!

Q: We know that. We don't believe him. Didn't you hear us tell him that he murdered you? So that means we believe you and not him. The truth is coming through. Peter is telling us the truth. Everyone is telling us the truth. Let's take deep breaths. If that's all you need to tell us, we think you need to go. We got it real clear. Most of the time John is saying, "No comment." Will you come back again, though?

MM: Yes.

Q: We need to run a lot of stuff by you. You need to be calm. Is it time for you to go, Marilyn?

MM: (No response.)

Goodbye, Marilyn.

Keeping with the theme of a rather active and surprising evening, another presence was felt on the board immediately. The letters GM HI were spelled out. Apparently, Gladys Mortenson (Baker) was back with us.

Q: Is there anything you can tell us that would help right now? Can you tell us what just happened? Did you tell Marilyn that John was here?

GB: Yes.

Q: Why did you go tell her? Did you want her to see John?

GB: Sorry.

Q: Are you sorry because she got so upset at seeing John?

GB: Yes.

Q: Can you tell us why Marilyn got so upset? Was it because of what John was saying?

GB: Yes.

Q: Because he had no remorse?

GB: Yes. He God damn lies!

Q: What lies? He just didn't answer our questions. He just wasn't telling the truth.

GB: Yes.

Q: In other words, when you went to tell Marilyn that John was here, you just told her, but you didn't come here with her.

GB: Yes.

Q: Let us ask you something. Can you say "God damn" where you are?

GB: Yes.

Q: There is nobody there to oversee you or correct you?

141

GB: No.

Q: What level are you on, Gladys?

GB: Gorgeous people!

Q: Is your mentality the same there as it was when you were here?

GB: Yes.

Q: Does that mean you still have a little instability?

GB: Could be.

Q: Did you try to wake one of us up last night? Was that you?

GB: Yes.

Q: Why were you trying to wake Lee up?

GB: Lonely.

Q: Yeah, but don't wake us up.

GB: Why not?

Q: One other question, if you don't like Bobby Kennedy, how did you make contact with him to get him on the board?

GB: I told him he had to because I would be around him.

Q: Would that bug him? Scare him? Drive him nuts?

GB: Yes.

Q: But, you're not on the same level as he is.

GB: Don't have to be on the same level.

Q: Can you go to another level to contact someone?

GB: Yes. He can't stand me!

Q: If you know so much about him, tell us the date he died.

GB: 6/5/1968 [Verified as 6/6/68[13]].

Q: How is Marilyn?

GB: She ignores me.

Q: Does she still blame you for a lot of things?

GB: Yes.

Q: Are you going to check on Marilyn when you leave here?

GB: I might go see her.

SAM GIANCANA
May 24, 1908[14] to June 19, 1975

Sam "Momo" Giancana, suspected of being Chicago's most feared and powerful Mafia crime boss, was a flashy figure who lived a flamboyant lifestyle.[15] Giancana and Frank Sinatra were reported to be owners of the Cal-Neva Lodge (a casino/resort in Lake Tahoe, California). This lodge was frequented by Marilyn Monroe, Peter Lawford, and at an earlier time by Joseph Kennedy (John F. Kennedy's father).[16]

To some degree, our group had talked about the feasibility of summoning Sam Giancana on the board, but we had not come to terms with such a confrontation with the former head of the Chicago underworld.

In our minds we could not agree on just how we could converse with a man of his reputation. Should we approach him with the allegation made against him by investigator Milo Speriglio who claims Giancana was responsible for the death of Marilyn Monroe?[17] Should we ask him if he was involved in the attempt to hit Fidel Castro?[18] While these questions were being pondered on the evening of September 17, 1990, the Chicago king himself came onto our Ouija board. Now the ball was in our court!

With the agility of a spider monkey and the fervor of a mountain lion, an entity identifying itself as Sam Giancana seemed to pounce on our Ouija board soon after some disoriented, and seemingly lonely, spirit tried to interject some irrelevant conversation.

The letters SG were spelled out on the board.

Q: Give us your birth date.
SG: 1908. [Verified]
Q: Is this a year—1908?
SG: Yes.
Q: What is the date of your death?
SG: 6/19/75. [Verified]
Q: How did you die, Sam?
SG: Shot.
Q: Where were you at the time you were shot?
SG: Chicago.
Q: Where were you?
SG: Home.
Q: Were you sleeping?
SG: No.
Q: Explain how it happened.
SG: Kitchen.
Q: Do you know who killed you?
SG: Yes.
Q: Did you let them in?
SG: Yes.
Q: Were you into a discussion before they killed you?
SG: Yes.
Q: You were in the kitchen. Were you all eating?
SG: No.
Q: Talking
SG: Cooking.
Q: What were you cooking?
SG: Sausage.

[Note: During our usual follow-up research, we were quite surprised to discover that Sam Giancana was indeed shot while cooking sausage in his kitchen.[19]]

Q: Did you know Marilyn?
SG: Yes.
Q: What was your relationship? Were you lovers?
SG: Hell no! Money.
Q: Gave her money?
SG: Yes.
Q: Do you know about her death?
SG: Yes.
Q: Can you tell us what you know?
SG: No.
Q: Why not? Did you have anything to do with it?
SG: No. Higher power.
Q: Government?
SG: No.
Q: Spirit power?
SG: No.
Q: Mafia power?
SG: Yes.
Q: Did Marilyn try to call you the day she died?
SG: Maybe.
Q: Are you not willing to tell?
SG: Afraid.
Q: Can you talk to us about Marilyn?
SG: Yes and no.
Q: Can you tell us what you know about her death?
SG: Killed.
Q: Do you know who killed her?
SG: Men.
Q: Were they your men, Sam?
SG: No. Mafia.
Q: Mafia men killed her?
SG: Yes.
Q: Who ordered the murder?

SG: John.

Q: John who?

SG: You know damn well!

Q: Are you talking about John Kennedy then?

SG: Yes.

Q: Can you tell us who else?

SG: No, because I can't.

Q: Why can't you?

SG: Brotherhood.

Q: Is that a spiritual brotherhood that you are talking about?

SG: No.

Q: Mafia brotherhood?

SG: Yes.

The entity identifying itself as Sam Giancana continued to share with us the fact that he had no knowledge of the plans for Marilyn and that he was upset when she died. It caused problems within the Mafia when he found out about it. Two of the men were from Chicago, and Sam knew them. He said he couldn't give us their names, but when we asked if one were named Tony, he said, "Yes." We asked if a man named Dave had anything to do with it, but he responded with, "I don't know."

According to Marilyn (in Chapter V), Tony had been killed because of his involvement in a blackmail scheme. We asked Sam to shed some light on this. His men killed Tony because he was trying to blackmail John Kennedy without Sam's permission as head of the Chicago Mob. We asked if he would ever have given permission to kill Marilyn, and his reply was, "No."

Sam went on to say that Bobby Kennedy had actually called and hired them (the two Mafia men) and that Bobby and John were equally involved. Sam did not know if Marilyn had tried to reach him for help prior to her death.

Q: Is there anything you could say that would help us in writing this book about Marilyn?

SG: I was killed by Feds. Killed to keep quiet.

Q: Why? Did it have anything to do with the Kennedys and Marilyn?

SG: No.

Q: They killed you to keep you quiet?

SG: Yes.

Q: Quiet about what?

SG: Testimony.

Q: Did you have to testify about something? Were you killed before you had to testify?

SG: Yes.

Q: Was it about the Jimmy Hoffa deal?

SG: Castro.

Q: What year was this?

SG: 1960.

Q: We are talking about the Bay of Pigs?

SG: Yes.

Q: You were subpoenaed to give testimony?

SG: Yes.

Q: You were involved in trying to kill Castro?

SG: Yes.

Q: You know this is all very complicated. It seems like the Mafia was involved with the government and in Marilyn's death. Can you tell us anything at all that would attach a name to who was involved other than Tony?

SG: We take care of our own.

Q: Was the Mob involved in killing John Kennedy?

SG: Yes and no. Bobby.

Q: The Mob was involved in killing Bobby?

SG: Yes.

Immediately after this question, we attempted to continue quizzing this entity to no avail. Perhaps we were once again getting into an area that was not meant for us to enter at this time. Sam Giancana was now gone from our Ouija board, leaving us once again to ponder the magnitude of these disclosures.

CHAPTER VIII

CONCLUSION

Thirty years after the death of Marilyn Monroe, the speculation continues. Her friends have been interviewed, and information and files have been examined and reexamined. And yet, the mystery endures. Did she commit suicide? Was it murder? Was it a lethal injection? Were records distorted, altered, or destroyed? Was there a cover-up? Was it politically or personally motivated? Who was involved? Our government and its agencies, organized crime, former lovers . . . all of the above? There has been no end to the speculation.

It is safe to say that Marilyn Monroe got caught up in a situation much more powerful than she. On February 18, 1991, we attempted to put to rest this tormented soul whose very substance wept, contending that an injustice was perpetrated against her.

Chapters III through VII contain information that the authors received directly from spirit communica-

149

tion. We cannot know how or why we were chosen to receive this startling information. However, once channels were established with our ethereal informants, we quickly became so familiar with them that we could recognize their individual styles. We found that we were able to distinguish which entity was communicating with us on the Ouija board by the way the planchette moved (pressure, speed, flow), coupled with their individual use of the language and phrasing. Almost all of the personal information given to us in these sessions was later verified through extensive research—birth and death dates, names of family members, and even unusual events such as Giancana's death.

During our research, we ran across a fascinating piece of information in Bernard Gittelson's *Intangible Evidence*[1]. There was mention of a *20/20* television episode dealing with the purported cover-up of Marilyn Monroe's death. This program was suddenly canceled by ABC in late 1985. Rumors were that Roone Arledge, who was then the president of ABC News, canceled the show at the last minute, perhaps out of his friendship with the Kennedy family.

Gittelson was discussing psychic Clarisa Bernhardt and her friendship with Bob Slatzer, who was married to Marilyn Monroe briefly in October 1952. Years before Marilyn's death, another psychic had told Slatzer that she (Marilyn) would be murdered. Later, in 1982, Mr. Slatzer pressured Los Angeles County to reopen its investigation of Marilyn's death. At that time, psychic Bernhardt told Slatzer, "I hate to tell you this, but there is just going to be another massive cover-up. But it's not over yet. Something else will come up in the next couple of years." [Gittelson, 1987, p. 173[2]]

Three years passed, and Slatzer was working with 20/20 on the Marilyn Monroe special. He talked again with Bernhardt, who predicted that the special would not be aired. However, "Clarisa still feels that there will be an investigation, owing to new evidence that has yet to come to light." [Gittelson, 1987, p. 137[3]] Perhaps our book will be a contributing factor.

We firmly believe that the information presented in our book sheds new light on a complex tragedy. And even as detailed as this information is, questions remain. It is a proven fact that in life, depending on the observer, inconsistencies in the description of events often occur. This phenomena evidently continues after death, as these individual entities' stories do not always agree. For example, still confusing us is the purpose of Marilyn's broken window, and it is difficult to believe that spiritualists have never tried to contact the late JFK. The incidents just after Marilyn's death are still hard to grasp. Where, how many times, and by whom was her body moved? And then there are the discrepancies surrounding the different ambulances that came to her house. Finally, it is difficult for most people to comprehend the magnitude of such a murderous scheme and the amount of power, intimidation, and fear brought to bear in order to cover it up.

After evaluating the results of the contacts we had with Marilyn and other entities that were allowed to converse with us, we were disturbed by their disclosures. We were aware of the fact that we are a small group of people suddenly burdened with the accounts of a murder that happened some twenty-nine years ago. We seemed to have only two choices. We could collect the information, box it, and put it away for future discussions. Or we could document it, put it in a readable format, and present it to the public for evaluation. Opinions were numerous. We were told that no one would believe the messages. We were also told that we would be accused of doing the work of the devil, and we were cautioned about opposing the so-called "establishment," along with the monied and powerful people in our country. In spite of these warnings, we did what the spirits asked of us, which was to disclose these communications.

Generally speaking, the public's attitude toward the parapsychological seems to be changing—opening up to an awareness of other aspects of reality. More people are accepting the premise that communication between living and discarnate beings is possible. It is conceivable that there are spirits all around us, existing as some form of energy—possibly in another dimension. With the advent of outer space exploration and interplanetary travel, the concept of a heaven just above the clouds has become extinct. It is our belief that while there may be a heaven, other dimensions run parallel to this one.

It is important for people to understand that those on the "other side" do not have all the answers. So, we are left, not with solid conclusions, evidence, or proof, but rather with an intangible explanation from beyond.

FAREWELL
AN EPILOGUE

We met on the evening of February 18, 1991, to wish our spirit friends peace and spiritual advancement. Our collective mood was good, and we had a special dinner planned, including place cards for all the entities with whom we had communicated.

Our greatest hope was that either Marilyn or Peter would be able to materialize to us, and we would be able to capture their images on our video recorder. After dinner and a champagne toast, we gathered around the Ouija board for a farewell contact, hoping that some, if not all, of the entities would meet with us this final time.

We did have a visit with Peter, Marilyn, John and Bobby Kennedy, Sam Giancana, and Gladys. We learned that Peter "plead the case" before a higher power in order to bring about tonight's gathering.

However, it soon became apparent that the mood of our guests was very different from before. For instance, Bobby had nothing to say, John was polite but let us know he only agreed to say goodbye out of his friendship with Peter. Giancana wanted to say only that he had nothing to do with Marilyn's murder. Gladys, rather than being pesky and addled, was angry, accusing us of having no respect for her.

Peter was not witty and flirtatious as usual, but seemed stressed by the responsibility he had undertaken in arranging this final meeting. He realized it was necessary for him to move on.

By contrast, Marilyn was not eager nor even willing to leave. She extended her time with us, amusing us by appearing to Lee and attempting to touch the back of our necks each in turn. None of us felt the touches, and nothing appeared on our video tape. To assure us that she had come to know us intimately, Marilyn also revealed a personal detail in each of our private lives that the other group members would have no way of knowing.

Marilyn was clearly upset at having to say goodbye. She said, "I could cry" and that she'd be back again in another life. Each time we said goodbye, she responded with yet another anecdote or amusing comment to keep us engaged. We urged her to move on, and she finally agreed.

In spite of our final farewell that night, Marilyn has continued to try to reestablish contact with us. She has appeared in our dreams, awakened us from sleep, and still plays on our emotions. We continue to be lovingly firm in our wishes to see her move on.

SESSION DATES

Chapter III: April 19, 1990; June 8, 1990; June 15, 1990; June 17, 1990; June 18, 1990; July 2, 1990; July 16, 1990; July 23, 1990; August 14, 1990; November 19, 1990.

Chapter IV: June 8, 1990; June 15, 1990; June 17, 1990; June 18, 1990; July 2, 1990; July 16, 1990; August 14, 1990; October 15, 1990; November 19, 1990.

Chapter V: June 8, 1990; June 15, 1990; June 18, 1990; July 2, 1990; August 14, 1990; November 19, 1990.

Chapter VI: July 27, 1990; August 20, 1990; September 10, 1990; October 15, 1990; December 1, 1990.

Chapter VII: August 5, 1990; August 20, 1990; August 27, 1990; September 3, 1990; September 17, 1990.

Farewell: February 18, 1991.

Afterword

THE LIFE AND LEGEND OF A GODDESS

We have never wanted our gods and goddesses to die. They are larger than life and thus provide us with intimations of our own immortality. Our modern deities, who appear as mesmerizing projections from the magic lantern of cinema, seem to have mastered omnipresence and to have eternal life. They have broken free of time and space and are able to materialize forever for our pleasure and inspiration. But even though we may have captured their images on film and seemingly broken the relentless clasp of time in order to achieve their everlasting existence, there is both an inordinate sorrow and an angry sense of loss when we learn that the actual physical body of the diety has been taken from us before we were prepared to release it. Once the corporeal form has been removed, we must cherish and perpetuate the legend.

Since 1962, Marilyn Monroe's legend as the abused

child and the used woman, the glamour queen who could never achieve personal happiness, has served as a symbol of the tormented celebrity who commits suicide after enduring more acclaim, adulation, envy, contempt, pity, and persecution than the psyche can tolerate.

Country star Loretta Lynn told a reporter for *Rolling Stone* that at one point in her career she had become so despondent because of the terrible pain she suffered from migraines that she briefly considered committing suicide, "just like Marilyn Monroe." The famous "coal miner's daughter" confessed that she had decided that people were only using her.

"My family used me, my kids, my husband, everybody," she said. "I was just like a piece of machinery . . . I could have ended up like Marilyn."

The child who would one day become Marilyn Monroe was born in the maternity ward of Los Angeles General Hospital on June 1, 1926. Her mother, Gladys Baker, a negative film cutter who worked at Columbia Studios, decided to christen her Norma Jean Mortenson. Although Gladys never married Edward Mortenson, an immigrant Norwegian baker, he received the title of father on Norma Jean's birth certificate. Tragically, however, the girl probably never knew him at all.

"I saw a photograph of him when I was around eight years old," Marilyn once told the press. "He was strong and manly, and he kind of looked like Clark Gable. He even had a little mustache. He died in a motorcycle accident in Ohio when I was only two years old."

The child could have used some of Edward Mortensen's Scandinavian stability instead of his Viking wanderlust. Norma Jean's maternal ancestors of Scotch and Irish heritage had neither money nor appreciable talents, and both of her maternal grandparents had died in mental institutions. An uncle, she learned years later, had committed suicide.

In numerous press interviews throughout her career, Marilyn Monroe always spoke about her family and her childhood in frank and honest terms. However, the essential problem to be found in her accounts was that she was rarely truthful about her past. Journalists who kept track of such statements soon discovered that she never hesitated to utter a new truth that might be completely contradictory to a previously attested fact. Although she often gave the appearance of extreme naiveté, vulnerability, and childlike innocence, she proved to be very clever in the manner in which she capitalized on soulful accounts of her mother's mental illness and her own deprived childhood. On several occasions, the actress made allusions to having been raped "eleven or twelve times" before she was twelve years old.

After Norma Jean's birth, Gladys Baker shared an apartment with Grace McKee, a coworker at Columbia, who came to love the child as if she were her own. It was Grace who later paid for Norma Jean's singing, dancing, and piano lessons.

Grace McKee remained Gladys Baker's loyal friend, even when she complained to their neighbors that she was slowly poisoning her to death. Gladys's mental deterioration accelerated shortly after Norma Jean's birth, and by the time the child was five years old, her hysterical outbursts caused her to be committed to an institution. Sadly, at about the same time, due to her own lack of funds, Grace McKee was forced to make Norma Jean a ward of Los Angeles County, and she was placed in the first of many foster homes.

Marilyn Monroe frequently addressed this state of miserable existence. She attributed the stammer that she developed at the age of nine to the trauma of having been raped by a boarder in one of the foster homes in which she had been placed. She detailed numerous other rapes and assaults she was forced to endure. She bitterly recalled the foster parents who abused her both psychologically and physically. She spoke often of her stay in the home of a religious fanatic who attempted to beat the love of God into her young body. Another foster parent provided so little food that Norma Jean had to steal from markets to stay alive. It was during such a foraging raid that a market owner caught the girl and forced her to have sex with him in a back room in order to avoid arrest.

Marilyn reviewed her childhood and found few times when anyone showed her any love, respect, or affection. "All anyone ever wanted was the monthly check they got from the county for taking me in," she said.

The faithful Grace, now married and named Goddard, visited Norma Jean when she was nine years old and living in the Los Angeles Orphans Home. Grace promised the girl that she would come to get her as soon as she could, but it was not until Norma Jean was eleven that Mrs. Goddard was able to make arrangements for her aunt, Ana Lower, to take the child. Miss Lower was a devout Christian Scientist, who was at last able to bestow some love and security upon Norma Jean. She also arranged for her to enroll in junior high school in Westwood Village.

This peaceful plateau was to last only a year before Ana Lower became too ill to care for the girl. Fortunately, Grace Goddard was at last able to bring Norma Jean home to live with her.

During this five-year period, Norma Jean had seen her mother sporadically, whenever she was released from a mental hospital. "She would be released because she was considered adjusted and ready to cope with the outside world," the actress said. "But always, within a few weeks, she would be back in confinement, institutionalized again."

By the time the well-endowed teenager entered high school in Van Nuys, Grace was experiencing great uncertainties. She knew that Norma Jean was subjected to a steady barrage of lewd and suggestive comments from the boys that followed her home from school each night. Neighbors told her that they were certain that her legal ward was cavorting in all-night beach parties. Grace was fearful that Norma Jean might replicate her mother's pattern of ending up pregnant and unable to cope with reality.

When Norma Jean dropped out of high school in February of 1942, Grace urged her to marry Jim Dougherty, a young man whom she considered the most eligible of her many suitors. In one of those little twists of fate so dear to all movie buffs, Dougherty worked at the Lockheed aircraft plant with Robert Mitchum, who would one day become a very popular actor and who would in 1954 co-star with Marilyn Monroe in *River of No Return*. Although their acquaintance was really quite casual in those frantic days of the war effort after the Japanese attack on Pearl Harbor,

Bob and Marilyn would later regale the press with nostalgic tales of their teenage friendship.

After their marriage in June of 1942, Dougherty never disparaged Norma Jean's willingness to enact the role of housewife. He remembered that she had been a "wonderful housekeeper who didn't have a lazy bone in her body." Later, though, when he became a physical instructor at the U.S. Merchant Marine base on Catalina Island, he began to find her style of undress quite disturbing. She proved to be a distraction not only to his men in training, but to his own ability to concentrate on his work. After all, she was a married woman, and she paraded about in a bathing suit, eager to pose for amateur photographers. And she seemed unduly flattered by the attention of strangers and the crass salute of a wolf whistle.

When Dougherty gave her a scolding for her inappropriate behavior and her revealing wardrobe, she merely shrugged that she didn't mind living in an all man's world as long as he let her be all woman in it. It surprised no one, perhaps least of all Dougherty, when the newlyweds separated a short time after their heart-to-heart talk. Norma obtained a divorce in Reno on October 2, 1946.

In the postwar years, the mass-market images of woman remained the same as they were prior to World War II. As before, woman was the glorified American sensual showgirl, the saintly mom, or the devouring vampire. The problem was, most men wanted the saintly mom on their arm in public and the sensual showgirl in the bedroom. And, if possible, they wanted both women in the same wife or girlfriend.

Norma Jean Dougherty seemed ideally cast as the

sensual showgirl, and in the months just prior to her divorce, cheesecake photographs of her ample charms began appearing regularly in many men's magazines. And as Dougherty had credited her industrious house-keeping, Norma Jean also proved that she didn't have a lazy bone in her body when it came to seeking out modeling jobs and posing for long hours.

Potter Heuth, a commercial photographer who spe-cialized in pinup pictures, featured Norma Jean in nu-merous layouts and brought her to the attention of Emmeline Snively, the head of a successful model agency. Here, Norma Jean soaked up every drop of pro-fessional advice made available to her. She was a sponge, absorbing all the tricks of the trade.

Emmeline Snively insisted that Norma Jean bleach her hair a lighter shade of blond. In a sense, it was she who created the physical image of the emerging entity who would become Marilyn Monroe. "That little girl worked," Ms. Snively commented. "A lot of models ask me how they can be like Marilyn Monroe. Honey, I say to them, if you can show half the gumption, just half, that that little girl showed, you'll be a success, too. But I doubt if there will ever be another like her."

In his book *Marilyn Monroe*, published two years be-fore her death, biographer Maurice Zolotow wrote of the actress's driving ambition: "In her heart is a quest-ing fever that will give her no peace, that drives her on 'to strive, to seek, to find,' and then to strive and seek again. Her soul will always be restless, unquiet."

Journalist Bob Slatzer met Norma Jean in the sum-mer of 1946. As a correspondent for an eastern newspaper, he was writing some feature articles on major movie celebrities.

"When we first met, Norma Jean was a model, trying to get steady work by making the rounds," Slatzer recalled. "We were both waiting to meet prospective clients in the lobby of Twentieth Century Fox studios when we struck up a conversation. We made a dinner date for later that evening."

Slatzer began a long relationship with Norma Jean that led to their brief marriage in 1952. "When we got married, Norma Jean was in the process of being transformed into the Hollywood Love Goddess known as Marilyn Monroe. Although she yielded to studio pressure and divorced me, we remained close friends until her death in 1962."

Marilyn's fourth husband, the acclaimed Pulitzer Prize-winning playwright Arthur Miller, had dealt with the manner in which the drive for personal success dominates American life in his classic work *The Death of a Salesman*. After Marilyn's death, Miller wrote *After the Fall*, in which the principal female character is generally recognized to be patterned after the legendary actress. When an interviewer for *The Paris Review* asked him if the girl in the play was a symbol of an obsession for success, Miller answered:

"Yes, she is consumed by what she does, and instead of it being a means of release, it's a jail. A prison which defines her, finally. She can't break through. In other words, success, instead of giving freedom of choice, becomes a way of life."

In 1947, Norma Jean's way of life and her successes were defined by the astonishing number of magazines that had published photographs of her remarkable face and figure. She was now a golden blonde, a golden creature, a golden goddess who promised every man's dream of endless sexual pleasure without the annoying consequences of real-life women. She was the ultimate fantasy projection with no threat of the annoying responsibilities that come with possessing a flesh-and-blood woman. She was a modern incarnation of the high priestesses of Ishtar, Asherah, and Aphrodite, manifesting there on glossy paper to dispense the power of the Great Mother through sexual worship and sexual healing.

From this point on, the saga of Norma Jean picks up a momentum that will not break pace until the terrible morning of August 5, 1962.

In 1946, the eccentric millionaire inventor Howard Hughes was convalescing in Cedars of Lebanon Hospital from injuries that he had suffered during a crash while piloting his private plane. A connoisseur of women as well as innovative aircraft, Hughes would shepherd such beauties as Jane Russell, Jean Peters, and Terry Moore into the Hollywood fold. But during this particular recovery period, he augmented his rejuvenation by ogling the suggestive photographs of Norma Jean that were featured in several current magazines.

"Find out the identity of this darling of the cheesecake magazines," he ordered the office staff at his RKO studios.

Within a few days, an associate from Hughes's RKO staff had telephoned Emmeline Snively, who, in turn, contacted Helen Ainsworth, an agent, and told her that no less a personage than Howard Hughes was interested in one of her models. After one interview with Norma Jean, Ms. Ainsworth was eager to represent her.

Wasting no time, Helen Ainsworth called Ben Lyon, the husband of Bebe Daniels and a Twentieth Century Fox talent scout. Lyon, who had himself been a popular Hollywood leading man during the twenties and thirties, appearing in such classics as *Hell's Angels* and *Bluebeard's Seven Wives*, responded as Ms. Ainsworth had anticipated when she mentioned that Howard Hughes was very interested in this exciting blond actress whom she represented. He arranged a meeting with Norma Jean at once.

Impressed with what he saw and recognizing the potential of the young woman's natural talent, Lyon decided to make a color test of Norma Jean on the set of a Betty Grable film, *Mother Wore Tights*. He also made the decision to shoot the test in the predawn hours and not to wait for the approval of the studio's boss Darryl F. Zanuck.

Three days after Lyon shot the color footage of Norma Jean, Zanuck viewed the test and set aside his pique that he had not personally authorized it. In August of 1946, while she was still officially Mrs. Jim Dougherty and only twenty years old, Darryl F. Zanuck signed Norma Jean to a players contract at Twentieth Century Fox. Within a week, she had been rechristened Marilyn Monroe. Six years later, with the release of *Niagara*, she had become an international cinema sex symbol. Twelve years later, she was in the process of being transformed from movie actress to screen legend. Sixteen years later, almost to the day, she was dead, officially listed as a suicide.

Maurice Zolotow has recalled his first meeting with the soon-to-be-famous Marilyn Monroe in 1953. The Los Angeles Press Club was honoring columnist Walter Winchell at the Ambassador Hotel, and Winchell was sitting at the head table: "On Winchell's left was [Darryl F.] Zanuck and on his right was a gorgeous blond woman in a very low-cut sequin, skintight gown. She didn't say a word. She listened to Winchell, who was a nonstop talker . . . She had a heavy layer of makeup and long fake eyelashes and enormous vermilion-lipsticked lips. She looked like the quintessence of the studio-manufactured sex body. She looked empty inside. She was Marilyn Monroe . . . She was about to become famous [in *Niagara*]."

The name "Marilyn Monroe" was a creation of Roy Croft, at that time a publicity man for Fox. Croft had always liked the name Marilyn because of his admiration for the musical comedy star Marilyn Miller. Grace Goddard, who had learned of Norma Jean's breakthrough with a major studio, recalled a bit of family history that had been told to her by Gladys Baker. According to Norma Jean's mother—unless it was all one of her fantasies—the Baker family had been distantly related to President James Monroe. Although Norma Jean accepted the Monroe part of her new professional name, she always disliked being called Marilyn. She had expressed her own preference for Jean Monroe.

But as many friends would recall, in those days the young actress didn't argue with anyone in any kind of authority. In those days when she was slowly working her way to better roles, she never questioned the opinion of any publicist or director. Neither did she have fits of temperament nor display embarrassing outbursts of angry emotions. Nor was she ever late for an assignment or an appointment. Few people would glimpse the tempest inside Norma Jean until she had truly become the Marilyn Monroe who sat in the driver's seat and wielded the whip of a bankable star.

The player's contract with Fox did not place her immediately in any kind of position of power, and Marilyn knew it. She knew that she had to toe the line or she would be back in her bathing suit and posing for the men's magazines. Always willing to go the extra mile in those days, she probably did not realize at the time just how arduous the trek to stardom would be and how long it would take before she received any kind of true public recognition.

As a starlet under contract, Marilyn continued to be used as cheesecake fodder for the newspapers and magazines. She was also utilized to decorate studio functions, attend movie openings on the arm of whatever mogul desired an attractive companion for the occasion, and, if the need arose, be on the set to serve as an extra or a bit player. For all of this, Marilyn received a modest weekly salary.

She was finally cast in two Fox productions, and film buffs will forever argue whether Marilyn Monroe's film debut was actually in *Scudda Hoo! Scudda Hay!* (1948) or *Dangerous Years* (1948). In either case, the actress's appearance in the production of a major studio is hardly auspicious.

Scudda Hoo! Scudda Hay! starred Fox's Number Two Blond Bombshell, June Haver (Number One was, of course, Betty Grable) and Lon McCallister. Accomplished character actors Walter Brennan, Anne Revere, Henry Hull, and Tom Tully were on hand to lend their support to this rustic melodrama of a farmer's son who seems to love his mules more than the lovely Ms. Haver. Marilyn's big scene came when she was to step from a crowd and say, "Hello, Peggy" to June Haver. Unfortunately, the dialogue sequence ended up on the cutting-room floor, and Marilyn can only be glimpsed in the background in a brief scene.

Dangerous Years featured two child actors Scotty Beckett and Darryl Hickman making the transition to more adult roles. The film itself was a quickie toss-off which portrayed the delinquent lives of teenagers who hung out in a juke joint. Marilyn was a carhop waitress with no dialogue.

Depression began to cloud Marilyn's mind. She was playing the starlet game to perfection. She was doing nothing to buck the system. She was even heeding the summons to the casting couch on what some friends would assess as a too-regular basis. In the words of one cynical director—who himself did not hesitate to exploit the young starlet—Marilyn was becoming the studio's sexual "filling station."

But all of this was to no avail. Fox dropped her option.

Part of the problem may have rested in the fact that she too greatly resembled the Queen of Twentieth Century Fox, Betty Grable, and the Heir Apparent (should Betty's gorgeous gams ever lose their appeal), June Haver. With one blonde supreme and a leading contender, Marilyn Monroe was the blonde most expendable.

Ironically, in 1955 when every studio in Hollywood was suffering from Monroe fever, blondes were measured by the Marilyn Standard, and the careers of such lookalikes as Jayne Mansfield, Mamie Van Doren, Di-ana Dors, Barbara Lang, Cleo Moore, Sheree North, and Barbara Nichols had their careers either lengthened or shortened depending on their ability to reflect Marilyn Monroe's inimitable style.

After her option had been dropped, Marilyn continued to attend the acting classes that Fox had initiated for her with The Actor's Lab, a school operated by Roman Bohnen, Morris Carnovsky, and J. Edward Bromberg. Specializing in the Stanislavsky theory of acting, the instructors at the Lab found Marilyn to be a great sympathizer, a woman who was able to project her fears and her dreams and to become one with them. They would later remember her as a dedicated pupil, and not the erratic child-woman with the nonexistent attention span that others would claim to recall.

Marilyn's agent Helen Ainsworth managed to arrange an interview for her with Max Arnow, head of the talent department at Columbia. Arnow viewed the color test that Marilyn had done for Ben Lyon at Fox, and he signed her to a six-month contract at a hundred twenty-five dollars a week.

It was in those early days at Columbia that Marilyn encountered acting teacher Natasha Lytess, the woman who was to become her mentor. Although Ms. Lytess would later admit that her first impression of Marilyn Monroe was that she was a simpleminded, vulgar, vacuous blonde, she soon found that the lovely young starlet's vacant stare masked a mind that was eager and willing to learn. Natasha's word on nearly every subject became a firm and absolute law to Marilyn.

For years to come, the actress would not consider herself prepared to do the most elementary film scene until she had worked out the fine points of the characterization to Natasha's satisfaction. And everyone, from directors to publicity flacks, would learn that the most effective manner of obtaining Marilyn's approval on any matter was to first obtain approval from Natasha Lytess. The acting teacher became Marilyn's personal adviser, as well as her drama coach, thereby giving rise to certain rumors that their relationship had become intimate on an even deeper level. Natasha would remain the dominant deciding force in Marilyn's life until she was replaced by Paula Strasberg of the famous Actor's Studio in New York.

In 1948, Columbia put Marilyn Monroe into her first starring film, *Ladies of the Chorus*, a low-budget musical that was designed to serve as a showcase for the blond starlet. Adele Jergens, who was only a few years older than Marilyn, played her mother, a burlesque queen who was fearful that her stripper daughter's rising stardom would squelch her romance with a socialite (Rand Brooks). Marilyn sang two songs, "Every Baby Needs A Da Da Daddy" and "Anyone Can Tell I Love You" that presaged the talent that would soon captivate a world of moviegoers. Marilyn had the capacity to come alive with the camera and to make magic with it.

Billy Wilder, who would direct Marilyn in *The Seven-Year Itch* and the classic film comedy *Some Like It Hot*, once commented on the similarities between Greta Garbo and Marilyn Monroe. Among several shared traits, he said that both women had an incredible capacity to create a special miracle between the time they stood before the camera and the time the film was developed and projected in the screening room. The miracle, Wilder insisted, happened somehow in the film emulsion.

What was it about their faces? Wilder said that they became all women—Eve, Cleopatra, Mata Hari. One could read into their faces "all the secrets of a woman's soul." It was "a strange trick of flesh impact—that is to say, their flesh registered for the camera and came across on the screen as real flesh that you could touch, an image beyond photography."

Garbo was notorious for her shyness, her desire for a private life. She seemed not so much to be eccentric as actually to fear strangers. Wilder stated that this was also true of Marilyn Monroe, "who dreaded people, who was a solitary seeker, who was only at ease with small animals and lonely beaches. Yet both [Garbo and Monroe] sprang to life when a camera was turned on their faces."

During the filming of *Ladies of the Chorus*, Marilyn fell madly in love with Fred Karger, the musical director who had arranged her songs. Karger, handsome, talented, and recently divorced, took a personal interest in the young actress, but he decided that he was not interested in marrying again.

Suddenly cold to her protestations of undying love, Karger arranged for Marilyn to move into the Hollywood Studio Club, a resident hotel for young women in the arts sponsored by the Women's Council of the Y.M.C.A. It was not long after Karger had become indifferent to Marilyn's infatuation, however, that he married Jane Wyman when her divorce from actor Ronald Reagan became final.

Stung by heartache over the loss of Fred Karger's love, Marilyn was somehow prepared when Columbia felt that she had not generated enough public response in *Ladies of the Chorus* to justify their renewing her contract. By now, her survival instincts were more finely honed than ever, and she had begun to cultivate people of influence in Hollywood who could do her career some good. Although Marilyn denied being anything other than platonic friends with such men of power as columnist Sidney Skolsky and Joseph Schenck, chairman of Twentieth Century Fox, there was no denying that she was experienced in using her sexual charms to get what she wanted. And what she wanted most of all was to become a star.

In 1950, two years after she had had a starring role in *Ladies of the Chorus,* her next cinematic appearance would be that of a walk-on in United Artists' *Love Happy,* which starred the Marx Brothers in what would be their last film. The part called only for a sexy woman to tell private eye Groucho that she was worried because men kept following her. Marilyn made the most of the walk-on—because no one could walk the way she could. Groucho and producer Lester Cowan were impressed by the famous Monroe hip action and her blond beauty.

The rather limp plot of *Love Happy* dealt with a group of down-on-their-luck actors who accidentally gain possession of the Romanov diamonds. Most of the action focused on Harpo, and Groucho and Chico had very few intelligible scenes in the entire film. When Groucho got a good look at the girl who was to wiggle in for the walk-on, he insisted that her part be lengthened enough to give him plenty of time to leer over his trademark greasepaint mustache and to raise his bushy brows in the famous Groucho double take. He wanted to milk the best scene that he had for all it was worth. Cowan agreed, and some additional dialogue was added to give Marilyn more screen time with Groucho.

Marilyn's bit part proved to create such an impact with preview audiences that Cowan arranged a personal-appearance tour for her in connection with *Love Happy*. The press had a field day with the stunning blonde wherever she appeared, and flashbulbs flashed like solar flares as photographers did their best to capture the Monroe walk on film.

Upon her return to Hollywood, Johnny Hyde, vice president of the William Morris Agency, met with Marilyn and made an offer to have his powerhouse firm represent her. Hyde became an immediate conquest for the twenty-three-year-old blonde. Thirty years older and suffering from a heart condition, he professed his love for her at the same time that he began to devote himself to her career.

Although Hyde was dead in less than a year from the time their affair began, close friends such as Bob Slatzer affirm that Marilyn did return his love. To the anguished consternation of Hyde's wife and children, Marilyn appeared at the funeral and threw herself on Hyde's coffin, hysterically proclaiming her love for him.

Before his death, Hyde had managed to get Marilyn a brief part in Fox's *Ticket to Tomahawk* (1950), which starred Anne Baxter and Dan Dailey. Intended as a sendup of westerns, most of the scenes that were written as satire were played with an awkwardness that created boredom rather than belly laughs. Marilyn was a corseted chorus girl providing part of an attractive background for song and dance man Dan Dailey's "Oh, What a Forward Young Man You Are" number.

Essentially unnoticed in *Ticket to Tomahawk*, Marilyn's two scenes in *The Asphalt Jungle* (MGM, 1950) made preview audiences sit up and take great notice. The buzz among the press was that she was the most exciting blonde to appear in films since Lana Turner.

Directed and cowritten by John Huston, the tough, taut-paced crime thriller starred such heavy hitters as Sterling Hayden, Louis Calhern, Jean Hagen, Sam Jaffe, and James Whitmore. Probably the first Hollywood film to show the planning of a major crime caper from the criminals' point of view, Marilyn was perfect in her role as the mistress of the crooked attorney (Calhern) who serves as the fence for the thieves. Countless hours rehearsing her lines with her mentor Natasha Lytess helped to make Marilyn a standout in the film. Incredibly, in spite of all the attention that Marilyn garnered in *The Asphalt Jungle*, MGM failed to offer her a contract.

Joseph L. Mankiewicz was quick to profit from MGM's oversight. A former MGM producer and writer, he was at that time ensconced at Twentieth Century Fox and very flush after winning Academy Awards in 1949 for Best Director and Best Writer with *A Letter to Three Wives*. Fully intending to keep his Oscars coming, he felt that he had another winner with his current project *All About Eve*, starring Bette Davis, Anne Baxter, George Sanders, Thelma Ritter, and Gary Merrill. In his opinion, Marilyn Monroe would be ideal as "Miss Casswell," Sanders' dumb blond mistress. Joseph Mankiewicz proved correct on both accounts: Marilyn once again caught the public's attention and he once again won Oscars for Best Director and Best Writer.

Marilyn's next bit part lacked both the class and the

sophisticated company of *All About Eve*. In *The Fireball* (Fox, 1950), she was an admirer of Mickey Rooney, who played a Roller Derby star.

MGM's *Right Cross* (1950) was another powerful crime drama with a stellar cast of Dick Powell, June Allyson, Ricardo Montalban, and Lionel Barrymore. Marilyn's contribution was slight. She was Powell's pickup date in a nightclub sequence.

Back to MGM for *Hometown Story* (1951), Marilyn was the secretary of Jeffrey Lynn, who portrayed a politician returning to newspaper work. Other members of the cast included Donald Crisp, Marjorie Reynolds, and Alan Hale, Jr., who would gain his greatest popularity as the skipper on *Gilligan's Island*.

Although her roles were small, Marilyn was beginning to attract more and more attention from the public and the press. When word got back to Darryl F. Zanuck that the exhibitors were more interested in the blond starlet than in some of their more established actors, he negotiated with the William Morris Agency and placed her under a seven-year contract. At the same time, he passed a studio decree that Marilyn Monroe was to be placed in any film in production or near production that required a sexy blonde somewhere within the plot line.

As Young as You Feel (Fox, 1951) had a good-natured script written by Paddy Chayevsky that spun a fantasy about an elderly employee who impersonates the president of the company in order to save the firm from bankruptcy. Monty Woolley was the masquerading employee, and the cast included a number of actors experienced in lighthearted farce, such as Constance Bennett, Thelma Ritter, David Wayne, and Allyn Joslyn. Marilyn was once again a secretary, this time to plant executive Albert Dekker.

In *Love Nest* (Fox, 1951), Marilyn finally got to say far more to June Haver than "Hello, Peggy," the line from her debut film *Scudda Hoo! Scudda Hay!* that ended up on the cutting-room floor. In this lively comedy, Marilyn was an ex-WAC who moves into an apartment house owned by a former army buddy, William Lundigan. Ms. Haver played Lundigan's wife, who suspected the worst concerning her husband and the blond mantrap who has become one of their tenants. Jack Parr, who would one day assume the helm of the *Tonight* show, was another of the screwball tenants.

Marilyn was becoming quite adept at playing the femme fatale in comedies, and she was learning a sense of style and pacing. In *Let's Make It Legal* (Fox, 1951), a slow-moving but effective comedy written by F. Hugh Herbert and I.A.L. Diamond, Marilyn enacted the lovely empediment who nearly stops Macdonald Carey from remarrying Claudette Colbert. Zachary Scott, Barbara Bates, and a very young Robert Wagner were also in the cast.

On loan to RKO, Marilyn managed to elevate her featured role in *Clash by Night* (1952) into star billing along with three of Hollywood's top guns—Barbara Stanwyck, Robert Ryan, and Paul Douglas. Although one critic labeled the romantic subplot involving Marilyn and Keith Andes as a kind of "Gidget Faces an Identity Crisis," the public warmed to Monroe's earthy wiggle. As an additional stroke of good fortune, *Clash by Night* just happened to be produced by Harriet Parsons, the daughter of Louella Parsons, empress of the gossip column. Louella began to say nice things about

Marilyn in newspapers throughout the nation, and the accomplished dramatic actress Barbara Stanwyck was not too proud to give the newcomer her due: "In a few years, we'll probably be supporting *her* in pictures."

When it appeared that Zanuck truly had a rising star in his stable, he almost singlehandedly slaughtered her career when he placed the new blond bombshell of Hollywood in *Don't Bother to Knock* and cast her as a psychopathic baby-sitter. Richard Widmark, Anne Bancroft, together with accomplished character actors Lurene Tuttle, Jim Backus, and Elisha Cook, Jr., were there to back her up, but it would have taken the U.S. Marines to have rescued the fledgling actress from such a monumental achievement in miscasting.

To make matters worse for Marilyn's soaring career, it was discovered that she had posed nude for one of photographer Tom Kelley's masterpieces of calendar art. The Fox publicity department desperately tried to suppress the story, and when that didn't work, they put pressure on Marilyn to deny everything.

Marilyn flatly refused. She explained that it was after she had been dumped by Columbia. She was broke, and she had rent and car payments to make. She accepted Kelley's offer of fifty dollars to pose, and that, she firmly stated, was that.

If that was that, Zanuck replied, he would shut down production on *Don't Bother to Knock*. But when the public refused to buy into what might have been a scandal to an earlier generation of moviegoers and began purchasing copies of the calendar by the ton, Zanuck and the moguls at Fox decided to review the situation. *Clash by Night* was doing big box-office business, and many theaters running the film were displaying only the name of Marilyn Monroe on their marquees. Production on *Don't Bother to Knock* was resumed and rushed into release.

Although the critics savaged the film, it was strong at the box office. The more gentle, understanding reviewers saw the role as most curious for a woman who had obviously been groomed to be a love goddess, not a deranged baby-sitter. And even though few people at that time knew that Marilyn had had close personal contact with a schizophrenic, a fair consensus maintained that the characterization was simply beyond her reach.

Zanuck knew that he had learned a lesson regarding his new star, but he did not yet know what that lesson was. As if Marilyn Monroe were a character in search of an author, he placed her in *Monkey Business*, a farce starring Cary Grant and Ginger Rogers; then immediately into an anthology film. *O. Henry's Full House* in which she costarred with Charles Laughton in "The Cop and the Anthem" episode.

It remained for *Niagara* to set Marilyn Monroe's star firmly in the Hollywood heavens. Fox publicists ballyhooed the film as featuring two of the wonders of the world, Niagara Falls and Marilyn Monroe. In fact, the movie, an excellent suspense tale, is marred only by an undue emphasis on Marilyn's wiggle as the color cameras recorded the longest walk in film history. In spite of this indulgence, *The New York Times* raved: "Seen from any angle, the Falls and Miss Monroe leave little to be desired."

Marilyn portrayed an unfaithful wife who plots to kill her husband (Joseph Cotton), only to have him turn the murderous tables on her. Jean Peters and Casey

Adams were a honeymooning couple who encounter Cotton. Marilyn sang one song, "Kiss," in her baby-doll voice.

Critic Pauline Kael found *Niagara* "compellingly tawdry and nasty," and "the only movie that explored the mean, unsavory potential of Marilyn Monroe's cuddly, infantile perversity."

It was while she was working in *Niagara* that Joe DiMaggio began his earnest courtship of Marilyn. DiMaggio, one of American's authentic heroes and legendary athletes, seemed to be just the proper kind of knight in shining armor for the woman who seemed to be rapidly ascending the stairs of the temple of Aphrodite to assume her mantle as the currently reigning love goddess.

With a bona fide American institution wanting to be her husband, Marilyn was able to enjoy a storybook romance. She received yet another satisfaction when she observed a significant changing of the guard. Zanuck, at last convinced of her box-office power, announced that she would be Lorelei Lee in *Gentlemen Prefer Blondes*, Fox's forthcoming extravaganza based on Anita Loos' popular musical comedy. It was well known that Betty Grable, for so many years the Queen Mother of Twentieth Century Fox, had yearned for the role and assumed that it would rightfully be hers.

Marilyn's costar was the statuesque, stunning brunette Jane Russell, who had become a national sex symbol in 1943 when she starred in Howard Hughes's *The Outlaw*. The film had run into so many censorship problems that it was not officially released until 1946 when a scissored version was finally approved. The resultant publicity had done nothing to blight the career of Jane Russell, who had gone on to star in such films as *The Paleface, Macao,* and *His Kind of Woman.*

A viewing of *Gentlemen Prefer Blondes* seems to indicate that Ms. Russell is determined to overpower the blond newcomer in certain scenes, but when Marilyn sings and dances "Diamonds Are a Girl's Best Friend" one can see that she is establishing her claim on the picture. And when Marilyn shares three musical numbers with Jane, including "Two Little Girls from Little Rock," it is apparent that she is not about to be pushed around by anyone. A critical consensus had it that although Jane Russell's prior Hollywood status demanded top billing, Marilyn Monroe stole the film with her sexy walk, her deadpan stare, and her innate comedic skills.

Marilyn was rushed into *How to Marry a Millionaire* (Fox, 1953), this time conceding top billing to Betty Grable. In *Gentlemen Prefer Blondes,* Jane Russell had been given the lioness's share of the lines and a meatier role. In *Millionaire,* Marilyn was given equal screen time with Betty Grable and Lauren Bacall.

The film, Cinemascope's first comedy, was assessed as being somewhat lacking in its dramatic reach, but most critics agreed that it was great fun. Marilyn proved once again to be an able comedienne, and Ms. Grable also turned in a remarkably effective comedy performance.

Ms. Grable, however, long the dependable workhorse of Fox and the possessor of the "legs that won World War II," was ready for semiretirement. Interestingly, at about the same time, June Haver, Fox's heir apparent to Queen Grable, married actor Fred McMurray and also retired from films. Marilyn Monroe was now the unchallenged reigning blonde of Twentieth Century Fox.

Eager to exploit the splendors of Cinemascope and Marilyn Monroe, Fox placed her next in *River of No Return* with Robert Mitchum. *Photoplay* magazine had voted her the best new star of 1953, and it was now that she began to feel that she had the power to do things her way. Famed director Otto Preminger cursed the actress for her tardiness, her demand to do endless retakes, and her insistence that each scene be worked out with Natasha Lytess. Audience acceptance of Marilyn as a saloon singer in rugged frontier times was mixed. She sang a number of songs, including the title piece, "The River of No Return."

Stung by Preminger's oath that he would not work with Marilyn Monroe again for any amount of money, the actress tried to defend her tardiness and seeming aloofness to columnist Hedda Hopper: "I'm not a quick study, and I'm serious about my work. I'm not experienced enough as an actress to chat with [people] on the set and then go straight into a difficult dramatic scene. I like to go directly from a scene to my dressing room and concentrate on the next one and keep my mind in one channel . . . All I'm thinking of is my performance, and I like to make it as good as I know how."

Fox decided that Marilyn should star in another musical, and it was with great excitement that they paired her with Frank Sinatra for *The Girl in Pink Tights*. Marilyn decided that she didn't even have to read the script to realize that the film had to be a rehash of two or three old Betty Grable movies. Although she told the Powers That Be at Fox that she would be eager to do a picture with Sinatra, there was no way that it would ever be *The Girl in Pink Tights*. When further discussion proved unproductive, Fox placed their new star on suspension.

On January 14, 1954, after two years of an irregular courtship, sporadic arguments, and many postponements, Marilyn Monroe married Joe DiMaggio in a judge's chambers in San Francisco. While honeymooning in the Far East, there were probably many times when joltin' Joe wished that he had a Louisville Slugger in his hands. Crowds mobbed them in Japan in a demanding manner not visited upon Yankee baseball immortals. Then Marilyn seemed to forget all about the honeymoon and accepted the U.S. Army's invitation to visit the boys in Korea. She returned to her groom's arms with a serious viral infection because she couldn't disappoint the G.I.'s huddled in that freezing cold by wearing her overcoat during her act. She well knew that the guys in Korea wanted to see what they were fighting for.

As a kind of wedding present, Fox told Marilyn that they would lift her suspension if she would appear in another big Cinemascope musical, *There's No Business Like Show Business*. Although the film included such musical comedy greats as Ethel Merman, Donald O'Connor, Mitzi Gaynor, Dan Dailey, and the popular singer Johnny Ray, Marilyn should have opted for Sinatra and *The Girl in Pink Tights*. The film played like a variety show's production of "Some of Irving Berlin's Greatest Hits." Although Marilyn's big musical number of "Heatwave" was one of the film's highlights, she was paired romantically with O'Connor in another of Fox's monumental miscastings. O'Connor, marvelous athletic dancer that he was, had, in such classic films as *Singing in the Rain,* always projected the image of the carefree eternal adolescent. To pair Peter Pan with the Earth Mother proved to be both silly and disastrous to the film.

Marilyn fared much better in her next film *The Seven-Year Itch* (Fox, 1955), which had been a successful Broadway production starring Tom Ewell. The picture was directed by the great Billy Wilder; and George Axelrod, the original playwright, rewrote a great deal of the play to better suit the talents of Marilyn Monroe. Ewell, who had been so accomplished on the stage as the man with the seven-year marital "itch," saw his part sacrificed to the glory of Hollywood's love goddess.

A charitable Tom Ewell remembered Marilyn Monroe essentially as a young woman with a "tremendous inferiority complex," who just "didn't think she was any good." Speaking with interviewer Charles Higham, Ewell recalled: "She wanted so desperately to be good that she found it hard to do even the smallest scene. She used to vomit before she went on before the camera."

Assessing the experience of directing Marilyn Monroe in its broadest sense, Billy Wilder remembered the shooting of *The Seven-Year Itch* with satisfaction. While it was true that Marilyn had often been late on the set, she was not *that* late. She did have some trouble remembering her lines, but she usually got them by the tenth take. Her procrastinations had caused production of the film to run three weeks late, but the transcendent quality of her work was worth such minor irritations.

What did annoy Wilder was her growing circle of

intellectual friends who sought to make of Marilyn something that she was not. "They're trying to elevate Marilyn to a level where she can't exist," he groused to Maurice Zolotow. "She will lose her audience. She is a calendar girl with warmth and charm. [Her circle of sophisticated friends] tell her that she is a deep emotional actress . . . Marilyn's whole success is that she *can't* act . . . If she takes it seriously, it is the end of Monroe."

Perhaps the single most famous scene in any of Marilyn's motion pictures occurs in *The Seven-Year Itch* when she stands on a subway grating and allows the air currents from below to blow her skirt over her head. Although the scene was filmed before dawn when the streets should have been virtually deserted, word of Marilyn's appearance had somehow leaked out and she performed the erotically suggestive scene before a very appreciative audience.

As fate would dictate, Joe DiMaggio had also received a message concerning the bedlam caused by his wife's naked thighs, and he, too, stood quietly in that rowdy, cheering, leering audience. He and Marilyn separated during the final days of filming *The Seven-Year Itch*. Nine months after their marriage, DiMaggio and Monroe were divorced.

Although the picture may have cost her a marriage, *The Seven-Year Itch* also sent her popularity soaring once again to the top of the box-office charts. Marilyn's interior workings told her that it was once again time to rebel. She told Fox that she wanted more control over her films. Among a long list of requirements, she demanded approval of script, director, and costar.

Darryl F. Zanuck snorted that to grant such demands would be to give her equal authority with him. He countered by sending her the script of *How To Be Very, Very Popular* and suggested that she begin work on the project at once. Marilyn refused to begin work on anything until Fox had capitulated. Zanuck once again placed her on suspension, summoned Sheree North, one of Fox's Blondes-in-Waiting, to assume Marilyn's role, and called Betty Grable out of semiretirement. But even the combination of two beautiful blondes could not match the star power of the current blond superstar. Critics saw the film as an ineffective "wacky remake" of the 1934 Bing Crosby/Miriam Hopkins musical farce *She Loves Me Not*.

While on her enforced sabbatical, Marilyn could often be spotted leaving airplanes and walking the streets carrying a copy of Feodor Dostoyevsky's novel *The Brothers Karamazov*. When reporters would inquire about the weighty tome, Marilyn would reply that it was her earnest desire to play the part of Grushenka in a motion picture version of the Russian classic. (The film was made in 1958 with German blond Maria Schell in Marilyn's coveted dream role.) While cynics believed the "Dostoyevsky device" to be nothing more than a intellectual ploy, perhaps inspired by Paula Strasberg, wife of Actor's Studio founder, Lee Strasberg, Marilyn continued to speak of her aspirations to enact dramatic roles of great depth. Later, after *The Brothers Karamazov* was cinematic history, she would state that her one great ambition was to play Lady Macbeth to Marlon Brando's Macbeth.

At the same time that she was strutting her independence and her budding intellectualism defiantly for all the world and Twentieth Century Fox to see, Marilyn moved to New York to form Marilyn Monroe Productions with accomplished photographer Milton Greene. Marilyn held a press conference to announce that it had been Greene's photographs in *Look* magazine that had convinced her that he had the perfect eye to capture her true self and that he possessed an instinctive knowledge of the kind of films that she most wanted to make. Marilyn Monroe Productions would create motion pictures of healthy and harmonious beauty and portray the actress as the sensual but wholesome and uncomplicated person that she truly was. They had acquired the rights to playwright Terence Rattigan's *The Sleeping Prince* as a likely initial production.

After fifteen months of holding out and generating a great deal of publicity for her own Marilyn Monroe Productions, Marilyn won her war with Twentieth Century Fox. In 1956, with a hefty boost in salary, she began work on *Bus Stop*, a motion picture based on the successful Broadway production by playwright William Inge. Paula Strasberg would be on the set to serve as her ever-present drama coach; George Axelrod was hired to adapt the script, and one of Marilyn's most admired directors, Joshua Logan, was brought in to helm the film. Although Rock Hudson turned down her offer to costar, she was pleased with her second choice of handsome newcomer Don Murray to play the naive cowboy who would pursue her Cherie, the tawdry nightclub singer. An additional benefit in choosing Murray was that although he would go on to appear in such critically acclaimed films as *The Bachelor Party*, *A Hatful of Rain*, and *Advise and Consent*, in 1956 he was an unknown who could not request star billing.

But even though Marilyn had won the control for

which she had fought and additional concessions had been granted in an effort to make the production run smoothly, she proved to be increasingly tardy and temperamental, not to mention grouchy and nasty. The compliant worker without a "lazy bone" in her body seemed to have disappeared for all time and to have been replaced by an actress who misused her power and abused those who sought only to help her achieve a successful film.

While she was portraying a disillusioned floozie afraid of love in *Bus Stop*, Marilyn had been falling in love with the playwright Arthur Miller. Although they had been seeing each other regularly for quite some time, they had managed to keep their relationship relatively quiet until Miller's divorce from his wife Mary Grace Slattery was settled. Once Miller was free to reveal his feelings for Marilyn, the press delighted in taking photographs and telling tales about the "Beauty and the Brain."

Marilyn oozed childlike love and admiration for her "brilliant, kind, sweet, wonderful" man and announced to the world that she had never been happier in her entire life. She would even become a convert to Judaism in order to help insure their complete and total happiness.

The week before their marriage, Miller had been invited to Washington, D.C., to discuss his alleged former affiliation with the Communist Party with the House Un-American Activities Committee. It was then that the Pulitzer Prize-winning playwright truly learned the incredible power that motion pictures work on the collective American psyche.

"I don't think they ever would have bothered me if it

hadn't been for Marilyn," Miller told an interviewer for *The Paris Review*. "And, in fact, I was told on good authority that the then chairman, Francis Walter, said that if Marilyn would take a photograph with him, shaking his hand, he would call off the whole thing."

Marilyn Monroe and Arthur Miller were married in a double-ring ceremony performed by Rabbi Robert Goldberg in White Plains, New York, on June 29, 1956. And then, strangely, just as she had combined her honeymoon with Joe DiMaggio to coincide with her tour of the Orient and G.I. bases in Korea, she timed her honeymoon with Miller to travel to Great Britain to begin *The Prince and the Showgirl* with Laurence Olivier.

The Sleeping Prince by Terence Rattigan, the initial property of Marilyn Monroe Productions, had become *The Prince and the Showgirl* (Warner Brothers/Marilyn Monroe Productions 1957). Somehow, in a moment of weakness or avarice, Laurence Olivier had agreed to direct and to costar in the film, but when Marilyn and her entourage arrived in England, he found that he utterly deplored every aspect of the entire production. Olivier worked like a man possessed to get the film completed on schedule so that he could be done with it.

The storyline was simple: While in London for the 1911 coronation of George V, a Carpathian prince picks up an American chorus girl, and the two very different people come to understand and respect each other. Some critics found the film very heavy-going and weak both in its comedy and its dramatic style. Others stated that *The Prince and the Showgirl* contained Marilyn Monroe's very best work.

During the summer of 1958, while she and Arthur

Miller were living on Long Island, Marilyn announced that she was pregnant. In July, however, she lost the baby and entered a deep depression. Arthur set about writing the original screenplay for *The Misfits* as a "get-well" present to his wife.

After *The Prince and the Showgirl* opened to lackluster reviews and corrosive critical attacks, Marilyn decided to dissolve Marilyn Monroe Productions and to terminate her partnership with Milton Greene. Milton of the magical eye and the intuitive touch, the man with vision who was to create harmonious pictures in which she might star with dignity, suddenly became the man who was attempting to cheat her, to work behind her back, to mismanage her affairs.

Greene protested that he had lost more money than he had made while in partnership with Marilyn. "I don't want to do anything to hurt her career," he stated, "but I did devote about a year and a half exclusively to her."

The divergent claims were quickly settled, and Marilyn began work on *Some Like It Hot,* the Mirisch Brothers' production of the Billy Wilder film that would become a milestone of motion picture comedy. With such costars as Jack Lemmon and Tony Curtis playing musicians fleeing the mob in women's clothing and joining an all-girl band, the Wilder-I.A.L. Diamond script was milked for every possible laugh. Although her interpretation of Sugar Kane, the delightfully ditzy nightclub singer, surely must rank among her very best performances, Marilyn's tantrums, truancies, and interminable retakes caused the film to take six weeks longer than scheduled to shoot and slam-dunked the budget almost a million dollars beyond the bottom line.

Although he had survived her eccentricities three years before on *The Seven-Year Itch*, Wilder found that Marilyn had become a "monster of monsters." Never had he encountered a performer who was so unreliable in her working habits. How could anyone consistently be several hours late on a shooting schedule and expect the film to finish anywhere near on time?

Maurice Zolotow stated that Tony Curtis made no secret of his contempt for Marilyn. "[Curtis] described the torment of waiting interminably for her. On her good days . . . she would come at eleven A.M. when there was a nine A.M. call. On her bad days, which was most of the time, she did not appear until after the lunch break."

Perhaps Norma Jean herself was becoming a bit weary of being Marilyn Monroe. The extraordinary French actress Simone Signoret, who won an Oscar for her performance in the British film *Room at the Top*, came to know Marilyn as a woman who rarely wore makeup and who spent her nonworking hours in a rayon dressing gown that she had picked up at Woolworth's. According to Ms. Signoret, the actress loathed the process of getting into her "Marilyn makeup." Marilyn complained that her legs were too short, her knees too knobby. And the trademark platinum blond hair came to be her special nemesis.

"Curiously, the roots of that hair, fluffy as the hair of a small child, didn't take the platinum dye as well as the rest of the hair on her blond head," Ms. Signoret said. "The lock that fell over her eye so casually and so accidentally was produced by all that teasing, and it was a shield protecting those darker roots, which might be seen when the camera came in for closeups."

On the set of *Some Like It Hot*, Tony Curtis recalled that Marilyn did not begin warming up until after the tenth take. On many scenes she required thirty or forty takes. One went to fifty-nine. In their love scenes together, he complained that he felt as if he were kissing Hitler!

Arthur Miller, one of America's most distinguished playwrights, was pressed into the role of an errand boy who was sent to deliver Marilyn's messages to Billy Wilder and return the director's replies.

All hates and hurts were officially forgiven and forgotten when *Some Like It Hot* became the most popular motion picture of 1959.

In 1960, Marilyn returned to Fox for *Let's Make Love* as the unchallenged box-office champion. The film was a rather complex revamping of the 1937 Dick Powell and Madeleine Carroll Fox musical *On the Avenue*, but the French actor Yves Montand had been imported to add a bit of continental charm to the moderately sophisticated production. Evidently, Marilyn found his Gallic charm too difficult to resist. While Arthur Miller worked in New York on his screenplay for *The Misfits* and Simone Signoret, Montand's wife, returned to Europe to work on her own film, the two costars began applying the title of the film to their after-hours companionship.

In her memoirs, *Nostalgia Isn't What It Used To Be*, Ms. Signoret recalled how she had been thoroughly enjoying the Roman spring and her work on the new film, when she learned that her "pal," Marilyn Monroe and her husband, who were working together, were now living under the same roof" and consequently sharing their solitudes, their fears, their moods, and their recollections of childhood poverty."

Montand, Ms. Signoret, Marilyn, and Arthur sat down and tried to be civilized and sophisticated about the affair of the unfaithful marriage partners, and the four of them were often seen together making the Hollywood nightclub circuit in a concerted effort to squelch the rumors appearing in the gossip columns. As it turned out, none of the pain caused Simone and Arthur by their spouses' infidelity could be justified by the final product of Montand and Marilyn's film. Their love scenes in *Let's Make Love* set off none of the sparks that they had generated off camera.

A remarkable cast was assembled for *The Misfits*, the film that Miller had written for his bride: The King himself, Clark Gable, now a distinguished fifty-eight years old; Montgomery Clift, the intense, always interesting leading man; the superb stage and screen character actor, Eli Wallach; and the accomplished supporting actors Thelma Ritter, Estelle Winwood, and Kevin McCarthy. Top off a stellar cast with the acclaimed director John Huston, a script by the Pulitzer Prize-winning playwright Arthur Miller, hundreds of wild horses thundering past all that raw Nevada scenery, and how could anyone produce anything other than a classic motion picture?

Unfortunately, in spite of excellent performances by Gable and Clift, the critics were almost unanimous in their aversion to the pretentious, heavy-handed script, the tedious plot, and the scenes of overt self-pity. The motion picture-going public, who felt that such an assembly of popular actors could only produce a great film, felt disappointed, even cheated, by their being served angst, rather than excitement, with their purchase of a ticket. No one was surprised when Marilyn traveled to Juarez, Mexico, to file for divorce from Arthur Miller on January 20, 1961.

The Misfits was Clark Gable's last picture. He died in November 1960, before the film's release and the birth of his first and only child. As it turned out, *The Misfits* would also be Marilyn Monroe's last performance.

The Misfits had been a United Artists/Seven Arts production, and after the debacle in the wilds of Nevada, Marilyn agreed to star in *Something's Got to Give* for Twentieth Century Fox. The film would be a remake of the old Cary Grant/Irene Dunne comedy, *My Favorite Wife*, and Dean Martin would be her costar. He would be fun, thought Marilyn, and she might even get invited to join the famous Rat Pack.

However, after thirty-two days of shooting, Fox had less than ten minutes of usable footage. Marilyn pleaded ill health, depression. She was working on her problems, she said. She was asking old friends, such as Peter Lawford, to help bolster her morale and courage.

The executives at Fox were not buying her excuses or her troubles. They well remembered Billy Wilder's horror stories from the set of *Some Like It Hot*. In their own baliwick, the still-uncompleted *Cleopatra* was rapidly becoming the most expensive motion picture in Hollywood history due to the hijinks, dalliances, and delays of Elizabeth Taylor. They handed Marilyn her pink slip and hired Lee Remick to replace her. Ms. Remick was another lovely blonde and a most capable actress, but Deano declared that he wanted out if Marilyn Monroe would not be in the picture.

Fox instituted a suit against Marilyn in an attempt to recover the money that they had lost on the motion picture that she had forced them to cancel. In a pathetic blur of accusations, attacks, self-recriminations, and public pleadings for sympathy, the last days of Marilyn Monroe were like one of those old-style movie montages where the calendar pages flip by and we perceive an accelerated passage of time. Before anyone could slow down the fast-forward movement, Marilyn Monroe's own personal movie had ended.

At her funeral, Lee Strasberg spoke the following words as a part of his eulogy to a woman who had been his student, his friend, and a love goddess to the world: "Marilyn Monroe was a legend. In her own lifetime she created a myth of what a poor girl from a deprived background could attain. For the entire world she became a symbol of the eternal feminine."

—Brad Steiger
Phoenix, Arizona

NOTES

Chapter III

1   Vandor, Paul E. *History of Fresno County California Vol. 2.* Los Angeles: Historic Record Co., 1919.
2   Summers, Anthony. *Goddess.* New York: Onyx, 1986.
3   Riese, Randall and Hitchens, Neal. *The Unabridged Marilyn, Her Life From A to Z.* New York: Bonanza Books, 1987.
4   Summers. *Goddess.*
5   Riese and Hitchens. *The Unabridged Marilyn, Her Life From A to Z.*
6   Moritz, Charles. *Current Biography Yearbook.* New York: H.W. Wilson, 1959.
7   Summers. *Goddess.*
8   Summers. *Goddess.*
9   Summers. *Goddess.*
10 Summers. *Goddess.*

Chapter IV
1   The Reporters Special Edition. *Marilyn—A Case for Murder.*
2   Summers. *Goddess.*
3   Summers. *Goddess*, p. 394.

Chapter V
1   The Reporters Special Edition. *Marilyn—A Case for Murder.*
2   Summers. *Goddess.*
3   Summers. *Goddess.*
4   Summers. *Goddess.*
5   The Reporters Special Edition. *Marilyn—A Case for Murder.*
6   Summers. *Goddess.*
7   Speriglio, Milo. *Marilyn Conspiracy.* New York: Pocket Books, 1986.

Chapter VI
1   Summers. *Goddess.*
2   Lawford, Patricia S. *The Peter Lawford Story.* New York: Carroll and Graf Publishers, Inc., 1988.
3   Katz, Ephraim. *The Film Encyclopedia.* New York: Thomas Y. Crowell, 1979.
4   Summers. *Goddess*, p. 401.
5   Lawford. *The Peter Lawford Story*, p. 239–240.
6   *Sun.* Vol. 8, No. 37, September 11, 1990.
7   Lawford. *The Peter Lawford Story.*

Chapter VII
1   Riese and Hitchens. *The Unabridged Marilyn, Her Life From A to Z.*

2   Riese and Hitchens. *The Unabridged Marilyn, Her Life From A to Z.*

3   Riese and Hitchens. *The Unabridged Marilyn, Her Life From A to Z.*

4   Riese and Hitchens. *The Unabridged Marilyn, Her Life From A to Z.*

5   *Encyclopedia of World Biography*, Vol 6. McGraw-Hill, 1973.

6   Riese and Hitchens. *The Unabridged Marilyn, Her Life From A to Z.*

7   *World Book Encyclopedia.* Chicago: World Book Inc., 1973.

8   Riese and Hitchens. *The Unabridged Marilyn, Her Life From A to Z.*

9   Davis, John H. *Mafia Kingfish—Carlos Marcello and the Assassination of John F. Kennedy.* New York: McGraw-Hill Pub. Co., 1989.

10 *World Book Encyclopedia.* 1973.

11 *World Book Encyclopedia.* 1973.

12 *World Book Encyclopedia.* 1973.

13 *Funk and Wagnalls New Encyclopedia.* Mahwah, NJ: Funk and Wagnalls, Inc., 1986.

14 Giancana, Antoinette and Renner, Thomas C. *Mafia Princess—Growing Up in Sam Giancana's Family.* New York: William Morrow and Co., Inc., 1984.

15 Nash, Robert J. *Open Files—A Narrative Encyclopedia of the World's Greatest Unsolved Crimes.* New York: McGraw-Hill, 1983.

16 Summers. *Goddess.*

17 "Geraldo" (Investigative News Group), Part Two. Ad-Hoc Mystery Series, 1988.

18 Sifakis, Carl. *The Encyclopedia of American Crime*

—*Abbandando to Zwillman*. New York: Facts on File, Inc., 1984.

19   Nash. *Open Files—A Narrative Encyclopedia of the World's Greatest Unsolved Crimes.*

Chapter VIII

1   Gittelson, Bernard. *Intangible Evidence*. New York: Simon and Schuster, 1987.

2   Gittelson. *Intangible Evidence*, p. 173.

3   Gittelson. *Intangible Evidence*, p. 137.

BIBLIOGRAPHY

Davis, John H. *Mafia Kingfish—Carlos Marcello and the Assassination of John F. Kennedy.* New York: McGraw-Hill Pub. Co., 1989.

Encyclopedia of World Biography, Vol 6. New York: McGraw-Hill, 1973.

The Fresno Bee. Vol. 136, No. 24649, August 7, 1990.

Funk and Wagnalls New Encyclopedia. Mahwah, NJ: Funk and Wagnalls, Inc., 1986.

"Geraldo" (Investigative News Group), Part Two. Ad-Hoc Mystery Series, 1988.

Giancana, Antionette and Renner, Thomas C. *Mafia Princess—Growing Up in Sam Giancana's Family.* New York: William Morrow and Co., Inc., 1984.

Gittelson, Bernard. *Intangible Evidence.* New York: Simon and Schuster, 1987.

201

Katz, Ephraim. *The Film Encyclopedia.* New York: Thomas Y. Crowell, 1979.

Lawford, Patricia S. *The Peter Lawford Story.* New York: Carroll and Graf Publishers, Inc., 1988.

Moritz, Charles. *Current Biography Yearbook.* New York: H.W. Wilson, 1959.

Nash, Robert J. *Open Files—A Narrative Encyclopedia of the World's Greatest Unsolved Crimes.* New York: McGraw-Hill, 1983.

Riese, Randall and Hitchens, Neal. *The Unabridged Marilyn, Her Life From A to Z.* New York: Bonanza Books, 1987.

The Reporters Special Edition. *Marilyn—A Case for Murder.*

Sifakis, Carl. *The Encyclopedia of American Crime— Abbandando to Zwillman.* New York: Facts on File Inc., 1984.

Sperigus, Milo. *Marilyn Conspiracy.* New York: Pockett Books, 1986.

Sun. Vol. 8, No. 37, September 11, 1990.

Summers, Anthony. *Goddess.* New York: Onyx, 1986.

Vandor, Paul E. *History of Fresno County California, Vol. 2.* Los Angeles; Historic Record Co., 1919.

World Book Encyclopedia. Chicago: World Book, Inc., 1990.

INDEX